TRAGEDY IN THE CHURCH: THE MISSING GIFTS

A·W·TOZER

TRAGEDY IN THE CHURCH: THE MISSING GIFTS

Revised Edition

COMPILED AND EDITED BY

GERALD B. SMITH

CHRISTIAN PUBLICATIONS

Camp Hill, Pennsylvania

Christian Publications
3825 Hartzdale Drive, Camp Hill, PA 17011

The mark of ✝ *vibrant faith*

ISBN: 0-87509-424-4
LOC Catalog Card Number: 90-81205
© 1990 by Christian Publications
All rights reserved
Printed in the United States of America

94 95   5 4 3 2

Cover photo: © David N. Dixon

CONTENTS

PREFACE

A.W. TOZER, DURING HIS FRUITFUL preaching minis-try, was concerned about the spiritual short-comings of Christian churches.

His week to week preaching always displayed love, appreciation and concern for the church—the true body of Christ on earth. The pattern of his preaching revealed a consistent yearning that every assembly of Christian believers would realize its full potential for the honor of Jesus Christ.

Fifteen years after the passing of Dr. Tozer, Christian Publications first issued these sermons as the seventh volume in the *Tozer Pulpit* series. It was the first to deal exclusively with subjects related to the Christian church and the spiritual basis for its varied and continuing ministries.

As with the other volumes, we point out that Dr. Tozer's sermons are not to be read as textbooks in a doctrinal sense. His appeal, chapter by chapter, is more likely to be devotional and inspirational.

We are truly thankful for the continuing demand for Dr. Tozer's edited sermons, the only available source for his often-prophetic and incisive material since his death in May, 1963.

The Publishers

1

God's Eternal Work: Only by His Spirit

". . . he . . . gave gifts to men." . . . he . . . gave some to be apostles, some to be prophets, some to be evangelists, and some to be pastors and teachers, to prepare God's people for works of service, so that the body of Christ may be built up. (Ephesians 4:8–12)

THE BIBLICAL TEACHING THAT GOD'S WORK through the church can be accomplished only by the energizing of the Holy Spirit is very hard for us humans to accept. It is a fact that frustrates our carnal desire for honor and praise, for glory and recognition.

Basically, God has been very kind and tender toward us. But there is no way in which He can compromise with our human pride and carnality. That is why His Word bears down so hard on "proud flesh," insisting that we understand and confess that no human gifts, no human talents can accomplish the ultimate and eternal work of God.

Even though God faithfully reminds us that a ministry of the Holy Spirit is to hide the Christian worker in the work, the true humility He seeks among us is still too often the exception and not the rule. We might as well confess that many have been

converted to Christ and have come into the church
without renouncing that human desire for honor
and praise. As a result, some have actually spent
lifetimes in religious work doing little more than
getting glory for themselves.

But the glory can belong only to God. If we take
the glory, God is being frustrated in the church.

With that background in mind, consider what
Jesus Christ actually did. He gave special gifts in
order "to prepare God's people for works of service, so that the body of Christ may be built up."
The ministry that the saints are to do—and the reference is not just to ordained ministers as we know
them—will bring about the building up of the body
of Christ "until we all reach unity in the faith and in
the knowledge of the Son of God and become mature, attaining to the whole measure of the fullness
of Christ" (Ephesians 4:13).

Some things are missing

It is rather common for visitors to my church to
ask me about some of the things they do not find
there. They want to know why my church frowns
on some customs found in other contemporary
groups. I try very hard to keep from drawing un-
complimentary comparisons with other churches.
If other churches fail to meet the high spiritual
standards God has set in His Word, they must answer to the Lord of the church. I am responsible
before God for the conduct of the work He has
given me to do.

I have prayerfully studied the Scriptures to determine how I can fit into God's program for accomplishing His eternal work. I find three basic re-

quirements God makes of the body of Christ if it is to do His final work—His eternal work.

First, Christian believers and Christian congregations must be thoroughly consecrated to Christ's glory alone. This means absolutely turning their backs on the contemporary insistence on human glory and recognition. I have done everything I can to keep "performers" out of my pulpit. I was not called to recognize "performers." I am confident our Lord never meant for the Christian church to provide a kind of religious stage where performers proudly take their bows, seeking personal recognition. That is not God's way to an eternal work. He has never indicated that proclamation of the gospel is to be dependent on human performances.

Instead, it is important to note how much the Bible has to say about the common people—the plain people. The Word of God speaks with such appreciation of the common people that I am inclined to believe they are especially dear to Him. Jesus was always surrounded by the common people. He had a few "stars," but largely His helpers were from the common people—the good people and, surely, not always the most brilliant.

Jesus looked first for consecration. In our own day it is certainly true that the Spirit of God uses those who are no longer interested in their own promotion but are dedicated to one thought: getting glory for Jesus Christ, who is Savior and Lord.

We are simply God's instruments

To please God, a person must be just an instrument for God to use. For a few seconds, picture in your mind the variety of wonderful and useful appliances we have in our homes. They have been engineered and built to perform tasks of all kinds. But without the inflow of electrical power they are just lumps of metal and plastic, unable to function and serve. They cannot do their work until power is applied from a dynamic outside source.

So it is in the work of God in the church. Many people preach and teach. Many take part in the music. Certain ones try to administer God's work. But if the power of God's Spirit does not have freedom to energize all they do, these workers might just as well stay home.

Natural gifts are not enough in God's work. The mighty Spirit of God must have freedom to animate and quicken with His overtones of creativity and blessing.

There have been in the past great preachers who were in demand all over the world. I think of one – a contemporary – a recognized divine in New England. He was not known primarily as a Bible preacher. He expounded on such subjects as nature and science, literature and philosophy. His books had instant sales and his pulpit oratory attracted great crowds. But when he died, the bottom just dropped out of all the work that had kept him so busy. He had given no place to the Spirit of God to direct all of that natural talent and energy. God's eternal work had not been furthered.

We may recall, however, that when Charles H. Spurgeon and G. Campbell Morgan passed away, their work and outreach went right on. Both of these well-known preachers had built their lifetime ministries on the Word of God and the power of the Spirit.

You can write it down as a fact: no matter what a man does, no matter how successful he seems to be in any field, if the Holy Spirit is not the chief energizer of his activity, it will all fall apart when he dies.

Perhaps the saddest part about all this is that the man may be honored at his death for his talents and abilities, but he will learn the truth in that great day when our Lord judges the work of every person. That which is solely his own work, accomplished by his own talent, will be recognized as nothing but wood, hay and straw.

The importance of prayer

A second important requirement if the believing church is to be used in God's ministry is prayer and the response God makes to our prayers uttered in true faith. This matter of prayer really bears on the great privileges of the common people, the children of God. No matter what our stature or status, we have the authority in the family of God to pray the prayer of faith. The prayer of faith engages the heart of God, meeting God's conditions of spiritual life and victory.

Our consideration of the power and efficacy of prayer enters into the question of why we are part of a Christian congregation and what that congregation is striving to be and do. We have to consider whether we are just going around and around—like a religious merry-go-round. Are we simply holding on to the painted mane of the painted horse, repeating a trip of very insignificant circles to a pleasing musical accompaniment?

Some may think the path of the religious carousel

is a kind of progress, but the family of God knows better. We are among those who believe in something more than holding religious services in the same old weekly groove. We believe that in an assembly of redeemed believers there should be marvelous answers to prayer.

We believe that God hears and actually answers our praying in the Spirit. One miraculous answer to prayer within a congregation will do more to lift, encourage and solidify the people of God than almost any other thing. Answers to our prayers will lift up the hands that hang down in discouragement and strengthen the feeble spiritual knees.

All of the advertising we can do will never equal the interest and participation in the things of God resulting from the gracious answers to the prayers of faith generated by the Holy Spirit.

Actually, it will be such prayer and the meeting of God's conditions that bring us to the third requirement if God is to fulfill His ordained accomplishments through the church. I speak of the Christian's dependence on the Holy Spirit and our willingness to exercise the Spirit's gifts.

An overflowing subject

This is an overflowing subject, one not easily exhausted, leading us into a consideration of the presence, power and blessings of God available only through the ministry of the Spirit. There are very few perceptive Christians who will argue with the fact that the gentle presence of the divine Spirit is always necessary if we are to see revival wonders.

I still have in my files an old sermon outline on

revival in the church. I preached on revival when I was young. I soon found out it was easy to preach revival sermons but very difficult to make them come to life in the church.

What do I mean by "revival wonders"? Well, you will find such wonders among the people of God when someone in the congregation steps out into a new and wonderful spiritual experience. Just let that happen to one young person and it will do more to cause the youth work to lift above the sandbar than a host of scheduled meetings and special conferences. The same is certainly true for older Christians. Just let one person step out in faith, claiming the fullness of the Spirit, crowning Jesus Christ as Lord, and the spiritual fallout will be felt by the entire group of believers.

We have to accept this as a spiritual principle, according to God's promises concerning the Holy Spirit. Such spiritual blessings cannot be bought. A true work of revival cannot be brought in by airplane or by freightliner. God's presence and blessing cannot be humanly induced.

Such revival wonders can take place only as the Holy Spirit energizes the Word of God as it is preached. Genuine blessings cannot come unless the Holy Spirit energizes, convinces and stirs the people of God.

Now, what does this all add up to? If we are intent upon God's glory alone, if we are using the resources of prayer and if we are obedient to the Spirit of God, there assuredly will be an attitude of true joyfulness in Christ's church. Those who know me probably do not think of me as an overwhelmingly cheerful man. But, thank God, I know about the true joy of the Lord and I believe we should be a joyful people.

All of us who are members of the body of Christ must face up to the question of whether or not we actually fit the description of "a joyful people." How many of us bring family and domestic problems right along with us, in thought and disposition, when we come to worship! How many business people bring their weekday troubles home on Friday nights and carry them along to church on Sunday!

We are children of the King

And what about the family's health? The worries about the children? How many of us continue to lug these problems and worries around on a full-time basis! We ought not to do it and we cannot be a joyful people if we do. Why should the children of the King go mourning all the day? Why should the children of the King hang their heads and tote their own burdens?

We are missing the mark about Christian victory and the life of joy in our Savior. We ought to be standing straight and praising our God!

I must agree with the psalmist that the joy of the Lord is the strength of His people. I do believe that the sad world is attracted to spiritual sunshine—the genuine thing, that is.

Some churches train their greeters and ushers to smile, showing as many teeth as possible. But I can sense that kind of display, and when I am greeted by a person who is smiling because he or she has been trained to smile, I know I am shaking the flipper of a trained seal. When the warmth and joy of the Holy Spirit are in a congregation, however, and the folks are spontaneously joyful, the result is a wonderful influence upon others.

I have said it a hundred times: The reason we have to search for so many things to cheer us up is the fact that we are not really joyful and contentedly happy within. I admit that we live in a gloomy world and that international affairs, nuclear threats, earthquakes and riots cause people to shake their heads in despair and say, "What's the use?" But we are Christians, and Christians have every right to be the happiest people in the world. We do not have to look to other sources. We look to the Word of God and discover how we can know the faithful God and draw upon His resources.

Another promise of God is that the Holy Spirit with His gifts and graces will also give us genuine love for one another. I am determined that I am going to love everybody, even if it kills me! I have set my heart on it. I am going to do it.

Some people do not like me—and they have said so. But I am going to love them, and they are not going to be able to stop me.

Love is not just feelings. Love is *willing*. You can will to love people. The Lord says to me, "Love people!" I know very well that He does not mean just to feel love for them. He means that I should will to love them.

What about sympathy and compassion?

It would be shortsighted to mention the blessed things the Holy Spirit wants to do in the midst of God's people and not add sympathy and compassion to the list. I dare to trust that you are sympa-

thetic toward your fellow Christians. I hope that
never do you hear of a fellow Christian being in
trouble or experiencing trials without feeling concern, without suffering over it and taking the matter to God in prayer.

This kind of concern for one another comes out
of love and understanding. If we have this grace by
God's Spirit, we will take no superior attitudes, we
will not be censorious of others. If the Lord should
take His hand from under us, we would plunge
down and be gone forever. We need to be keenly
aware of that. I thank God for His goodness which
He continues to reveal to us in spite of our many
weaknesses and faults.

It is in this context that I recall a conversation
with a devoted English brother, Noel Palmer—a tall,
expressive Salvation Army officer with a great
voice. "Brother Palmer," I said to him, "what about
sanctification in the heart? What does it mean?"

His response was quick. "I believe that if the
heart loves God and wants to do right, God will
overlook a lot of flaws—and He will give us light as
we walk with Him."

I say with Noel Palmer, thank God you do not
have to be flawless to be blessed! You need to have
a big heart that wants the will of God more than
anything else in the world. You need also to have
an eye single to His glory.

These are the things that matter: exercising the
gifts of God's Spirit by the energy of the Spirit.
These are the things that must be important to us in
our congregations. They all add up to the fact that
the Holy Spirit is making Jesus Christ our chief joy
and delight!

CHAPTER

2

The Gifts of the Spirit: Necessity in the Church

So in Christ we who are many form one body, and each member belongs to all the others. We have different gifts, according to the grace given us. (Romans 12:5–6)

There are different kinds of gifts, but the same Spirit. There are different kinds of service, but the same Lord. There are different kinds of working, but the same God works all of them in all men.

Now to each one the manifestation of the Spirit is given for the common good. (1 Corinthians 12:4–7)

THE GENUINE GIFTS OF THE HOLY SPIRIT are a necessity in the spiritual life. They are also a necessity for the ministry of every Christian congregation serious about glorifying Jesus Christ as Savior and Lord. On those two points the Bible is clear.

But having said that, I also must add that I do not know of any denomination or communion anywhere in the world that has come into full and perfect realization of the Pauline doctrine and goal of spiritual life in the believing body of Christ.

That is a conclusion that may not give much encouragement to the critical and restless ones who

13

seem to be found in nearly every Christian fellow-ship. They seem to be just perched and ready to fly away to more spiritual pastures as soon as they can locate a perfect congregation made up of perfect people and led by a perfect minister!

It seems to me that Paul in his letters was trying to make it as plain as he could that any segment of the body of Christ anywhere in the world should sum up within itself all of the offices, gifts and workings of the entire church of Christ. In short, any local assembly ought to demonstrate all of the functions of the whole body. Paul clearly teaches that each Christian believer ought to demonstrate a proper gift or gifts, bestowed by God the Holy Spirit, and that together the believers should ac-complish the work of God as a team.

Believers are the body of Christ

Let us review something here that we probably know: the doctrine of the life and operation of Christian believers on earth—starting with the fact that the Christian church is the body of Christ, Je-sus Himself being the Headship of that body. Every true Christian, no matter where he or she lives, is a part of that body, and the Holy Spirit is to the church what our own souls are to our physical bodies. Through the operation of the Holy Spirit, Christ becomes the life, the unity and the con-sciousness of the body, which is the church. Let the soul leave the physical body and all the parts of the body cease to function. Let the Spirit be denied His place in the spiritual body, and the church ceases to function as God intended.

Every human body is thus an apt illustration of

the spiritual life and functions of the church. Paul uses the analogy in three of his New Testament letters, thus indicating that it is more than an illustration. It is something carefully planned: members designed and created for distinct functions under the control of the Head, Jesus Christ. Illustrations are never perfect, and parallels will generally break down at some point, particularly when we come to the sacred and infinite things of God. For instance, for a person's physical body to function, the parts have to be in one place. Scatter those parts around, and the person is dead. But the body of Christ, the church, does not have to be in one place. It has a unity, the unity of the Spirit. Some parts are in heaven. There are parts in practically every country on earth. And yet the true church, the body of Christ, is neither torn nor divided, for it is held together by the Holy Spirit, who maintains the life of the body and controls the functions of the members.

In the illustration of the physical body, the parts are all designed for specific functions. The eye is designed for seeing. The ear is designed for hearing. The hand is designed in a most special way to perform distinct functions. The lungs are designed for breathing, the heart for the circulation of the blood. All of these are designed to cooperate and act in concert with each other.

So it is to be in the body of Christ. According to the Bible, the whole body exists for its members and the members exist for the whole body. And that, of course, is the reason God gives gifts, so that the body may profit spiritually and maintain

spiritual health and prosperity in its service for
Jesus Christ in an unfriendly world.

The head controls the body

Now, what about the control of the members?
This is the point that many people seem to forget.
All of the effective, cooperating members of the
body take their direction from the Head. In the
human body, when a person's head is separated
from the rest of him or her, there can be no more
control or direction of those members that had
functioned together so well in the past. This is
plain physiology: the physical body must get its
control and direction from the head.

It is just as plain in Bible teaching that the
church, the body of Christ, must get its life, its
control, its direction from its living Head, Jesus
Christ, our Lord. Every Christian, then, should be
vitally concerned with and personally interested
in what the Bible tells us about the functions of
the members. These functions—called gifts in the
Bible—are special abilities. They are gifts from God
out of the store of His grace.

Paul wrote to the Roman church this reminder:
"By the grace given me I say to every one of you:
Do not think of yourself more highly than you
ought, but rather think of yourself with sober judgment, in accordance with the measure of faith God
has given you" (Romans 12:3). Paul then makes it
plain that all believers in the church had been given
"different gifts, according to the grace given us"
(12:6).

Some teachers seem to think they know exactly

how many gifts of the Spirit are mentioned in the New Testament letters. But I say it is difficult to be dogmatic about the total number. It is certainly possible that some of the designations are synonymous with one another, such as gifts of ruling and gifts of government, and no doubt there is some overlapping in the varied gift functions.

In First Corinthians 12, where Paul writes about the diversities of gifts, nine are mentioned specifically. Later in the same chapter he speaks of God setting apostles, prophets and teachers in the church and mentions such other gifts as helps and governments. In Romans 12, Paul makes reference to the gifts of exhortation, giving, ruling and showing mercy. In Ephesians 4, he mentions the gift functions of evangelists and pastors.

The apostles were unique

It is generally agreed—though not by all—that the apostles (see 1 Corinthians 12:28; Ephesians 4:11) chosen by Jesus had a particular office which has not been perpetuated. They were personal witnesses of the life and ministry of Christ Himself.

The New Testament gift of prophecy (1 Corinthians 12:10, 28) was not to predict but to tell forth what God has to say and to proclaim God's truth for the present age.

We cannot deny that Christian teachers (12:28; Romans 12:7; Ephesians 4:11) should have a special gift. Let us not be afraid to admit that not everyone can teach. Even those with natural capabilities must have a special anointing from the Spirit of God to impart spiritual truth. This is undoubtedly true also of the special gifts of wisdom and knowledge (1 Corinthians 12:8).

The basic spiritual life within the body of Christ has always humbly acknowledged the sovereignty of the Spirit of God in gifts of healing (12:9, 28) and miracles (12:10, 28).

In First Corinthians Paul concludes his references to the gifts with the mention of "speaking in different kinds of tongues" and then asks the rhetorical question: "Are all apostles? Are all prophets? Are all teachers? Do all work miracles? Do all have gifts of healing? Do all speak in tongues? Do all interpret?" (12:29–30). The answer to these questions, of course, is no, for Paul then instructs: "Eagerly desire the greater gifts. And now I will show you the most excellent way" (12:31–13:1).

It has been suggested to me that all Christian groups that believe in the authenticity and necessity of the gifts of the Spirit in the church in our time should be able to stand together in a great unity of fellowship. I can only say here what I have often said to many of my friends in the groups associated with what is referred to as "the tongues movement." I do not believe it is proper to magnify one gift above all others, particularly when that gift is one that Paul described as of least value. In any setting, the tendency to place personal feeling above the Scriptures is always an insult to God. Where the wise and gentle Spirit of God is in control, believers ought to exhibit genuine discernment. In some "gifted" circles today, there is an almost total lack of spiritual discernment and a credulity beyond belief.

Make the proper tests

I certainly am not making a blanket condemnation of individuals or churches. But there are some who say, "We have the gifts of the Spirit. Come and join us!" Before I join a movement, a school of thought, a theological persuasion or a church denomination, I must make the proper tests. What have been the characteristics and the earmarks of that group over a long period of years? Is there an exercise of sharp spiritual discernment that knows the flesh from the Spirit? Is there an emphasis on spiritual cohesion and unity? Is there a scriptural emphasis on purity of life?

For our gospel-believing Christian circles in general, I fear there is an alarming lack of spiritual discernment. Because we have shut out the Holy Spirit in so many ways, we are stumbling along as though we are spiritually blindfolded. Ruling out the discernment and leadership of the Holy Spirit is the only possible explanation for the manner in which Christian churches have yielded to the temptation to entertain.

There is no other explanation for the wave of rationalism that now marks the life of many congregations. And what about the increasing compromise with all of the deadening forces of worldliness? The true, humble and uncompromising church of Christ is harder and harder to find. It is not because leaders and the rank and file within the church are bad. It is only because the Holy Spirit of God has been forcibly shut out and the needful gift of discernment about spiritual things is no longer present.

We definitely need the gift of faith (1 Corinthians 12:9)—and I do not mean that faith which we all must exercise to be saved. We need men and women with a special and peculiar gift of faith, which often links with the gift of discernment by the Spirit.

There is a simple gift function of helps (1 Corinthians 12:28). I do not know all that it means, but I know many Christians who are just to be helpers in the work of Christ.

Related to that is the gift of showing mercy (Romans 12:8): going about doing good and encouraging the discouraged, as Jesus did so often.

There is a gift of administration in the church (1 Corinthians 12:28), and it may be the same as the gift of leadership (Romans 12:8).

Giving is a gift

Some may not know that there is a true gift of contributing (Romans 12:8). All believers are to give—the Bible teaches that. But there is such a thing as a special gift of giving.

The Bible also speaks of the gift function of the evangelist and the pastor (Ephesians 4:11) in the church.

God has given us in His Holy Spirit every gift, every power, every help we need to serve Him. We do not have to look around for some other way.

The most solemn aspect of this is our individual responsibility. The Bible teaches that a day is coming when we must all appear before the judgment seat of Christ. At that time everyone faces a review of the things done in his or her body, whether good or bad.

In that day we will be fully exposed, and the things that we have done in our own strength and for our own glory will be quickly blown away like worthless hay and straw, forever separated from the kind of deeds and ministries that are Spirit-wrought and described as eternal treasures in the sight of God—gold and silver and precious stones that the fire cannot harm. In that day all that is related to the work of the flesh will perish and pass away, and only that which has been wrought by the Spirit of God will remain.

Do you dare to accept the fact that the sovereign God has designed to do all of His work through spiritually gifted men and women? Therefore, He does all of His work on earth through humble and faithful believers who are given spiritual gifts and abilities beyond their own capacities.

Let me shock you at this point. A naturally bright person can carry on religious activity without a special gift from God. Filling church pulpits every week are some who are using only natural abilities and special training. Some are known as Bible expositors, for it is possible to read and study commentaries and then repeat what has been learned about the Scriptures. Yes, it may shock you, but it is true that anyone able to talk fluently can learn to use religious phrases and can become recognized as a preacher.

True preaching is Spirit-gifted

But if any person is determined to preach so that his work and ministry will abide in the day of the judgment fire, then he must preach, teach and exhort with the kind of love and concern that comes

only through a genuine gift of the Holy Spirit—
something beyond his own capabilities.

We need to remember that even our Lord Jesus
Christ, ministering in the time of His humanity
among us, depended upon the anointing of the
Spirit. He applied the words of the prophet Isaiah
to Himself when He said,

> "The Spirit of the Lord is on me,
>   because he has anointed me
>   to preach good news to the poor.
> He has sent me to proclaim freedom for the
>   prisoners
>   and recovery of sight for the blind,
> to release the oppressed,
>   to proclaim the year of the Lord's favor."
> (Luke 4:18–19)

Do we realize that when leaders and members
of a church do not have the genuine gifts of the
Spirit—the true anointing of the Spirit—they are
thrown back to depend upon human and natural
capabilities? In that case, natural talents must come
to the fore.

We hear that some fellow can whistle through his
teeth. Someone else has marvelous talent for im-
promptu composition of poetry. Some musicians
are talented players and singers. Others are talented talkers (let us admit it!). So in this realm of
religious activity, talent runs the church. The gifts
of the Spirit are not recognized and used as God
intended.

Much of church activity and fellowship also falls
back upon the practice of psychology. Many church
leaders are masterful psychologists. They know

how to handle people and get the crowds to come. Their operation qualifies as an amazingly "success-ful" church. Part of the success of that church depends on people with business talents and part of it depends on people with natural gifts as sales-persons and politicians.

A Christian congregation can survive and often appear to prosper in the community by the exercise of human talent and without any touch from the Holy Spirit. But it is simply religious activity, and the dear people will not know anything better until the great and terrible day when our self-employed talents are burned with fire and only what was wrought by the Holy Spirit will stand.

God is waiting and willing

Through His Spirit, God is waiting and willing to do for any church what He wants to do for the entire body of Christ. It was the promise of Christ that "you will receive power when the Holy Spirit comes on you" (Acts 1:8). The disciples were taught that the Holy Spirit would also bestow sweet graces and pleasant fruits of godliness when He could gain control of their persons.

Let me share my earnest hope and expectation with you: I believe the Holy Spirit of God wants to do some gracious new thing in our midst! With the dignity and self-control that is basic to the Christian faith, with the calmness and sweetness that belong to Jesus Christ, with the abandonment that marked the spiritual life of the apostles in the early church, let us throw ourselves out on the great full-ness of God with expectation!

Would it not be a wonderful thing if that outpouring of the Spirit of God that came to the Moravians centuries ago would come upon us again? They could only explain, "It was a sense of the loving nearness of the Savior instantaneously bestowed."

Oh, what that would do for us—a sense of the loving nearness of the Savior instantaneously bestowed! With it comes a love for God's Word, loving cohesion, dignity, usefulness, high moral living and purity of life—because that is the only kind of nearness the Holy Spirit ever brings.

3

Tragedy in the Church: The Missing Gifts

Now to each one the manifestation of the Spirit is given for the common good. (1 Corinthians 12:7)

THE CHRISTIAN CHURCH CANNOT RISE to its true stature in accomplishing God's purposes when its members neglect the true gifts and graces of God's Spirit. Much of the religious activity we see in our churches is not the eternal working of the Eternal Spirit but the mortal working of man's mortal mind.

That is raw tragedy!

From what I see and sense in evangelical circles, I would have to say that about 90 percent of the religious work carried on in the churches is being done by ungifted members. I am speaking of men and women who know how to do many things but who fail to display the spiritual gifts promised through the Holy Spirit.

This is one of the ways in which we have slowed down the true working of God in His church and in the hearts of unbelieving people all around us. We have allowed members of the body who possess no genuine gifts of the Spirit to do religious work.

It has been gratifying in recent interdenominational conferences I have attended to fellowship with internationally-known ministers who are preaching about the great need for the Spirit's operation among the people of God. This conviction is being echoed and reechoed throughout the world as our Lord is confirming the same need to many thousands of Christians in denominations everywhere.

"Why this emphasis?" you ask. "Doesn't every Christian have the Holy Spirit?"

There is plenty of biblical authority to affirm that every regenerated believer has a measure of the Spirit. Paul reminded the Corinthian believers that they had been baptized into one body by the Spirit (1 Corinthians 12:13). He told the believers in Rome, "If anyone does not have the Spirit of Christ, he does not belong to Christ" (Romans 8:9).

But God has more

But in the same letter in which he explained to the Corinthian Christians the operation of the Spirit of God in their regeneration, Paul also told them: "About spiritual gifts . . . I do not want you to be ignorant" (1 Corinthians 12:1), and then, "Eagerly desire the greater gifts" (12:31). If Paul only wanted them to know that they had a measure of the Spirit upon conversion, he would have said that and stopped right there. But he went on at great length to explain the necessity for the functioning of the gifts of the Spirit in the church. And I believe he was explaining that these spiritual functions and capabilities are the birthright of every Christian.

Paul did not say we must be important and well-known Christians to be useful to the Spirit of God in the functioning of Christ's body, the church. This is not something reserved for the great. It is the birthright of the most humble saint.

Paul reminded the Corinthian believers that God actually was seeking the simple people because they were willing to respond to the outworking of God's plan through the Holy Spirit and His ministry.

"Where is the wise man?" Paul asks. "Where is the scholar? Where is the philosopher of this age? Has not God made foolish the wisdom of the world?" (1 Corinthians 1:20). And then he goes on to say, "But God chose the foolish things of the world to shame the wise; God chose the weak things of the world to shame the strong. He chose the lowly things of this world and the despised things—and the things that are not—to nullify the things that are, so that no one may boast before him" (1:27-29).

The Spirit of God, His presence and His gifts are not simply desirable in our Christian congregations; they are absolutely imperative!

Now here is another aspect of truth often overlooked. The regenerated, converted men and women who joyfully have found their place in the body of Christ by faith are still humans, even though redeemed through faith in the death and resurrection of Jesus Christ. Having found divine forgiveness through God's mercy and grace, they delight in the complete lifting of the sense of guilt and in the fellowship they find in varied segments of the visible church of Jesus Christ here on earth—here and now.

But they are still human

My point is this: They still are human and they are living in bodies as yet unredeemed. If they are to continue in the blessing of the fellowship of the spiritually redeemed, if they are to successfully engage in the Christian witness God expects of them, they must consciously know and experience the indwelling illumination of the Holy Spirit of God. They must depend upon His gifts, His enduement and His anointing if they hope to cope with the universal blight which is upon mankind.

Believers are yet in their unredeemed bodies. This is true of every believer, every member of the body, whether the oldest, sweetest saint of God who has followed on to know the Lord or the newest convert who has just found forgiveness of sins and the joy of salvation.

Yes, this is orthodox Christian theology, and this is how the apostle Paul revealed it to us:

> For the creature was subjected to frustration, not by its own choice, but by the will of the one who subjected it, in hope that the creation itself will be liberated from its bondage to decay and brought into the glorious freedom of the children of God.
>
> We know that the whole creation has been groaning as in the pains of childbirth right up to the present time. Not only so, but we ourselves, who have the firstfruits of the Spirit, groan inwardly as we wait eagerly for our adoption as sons, the redemption of our bodies. (Romans 8:20–23)

There is no other way we can have it. The saints of God in this age do live in an unredeemed temple. The body is potentially redeemed, for that is the promise of God. But in this life it is not yet actually redeemed. And that is why it is impossible for God to use men and women, who yet must die, to bring about His eternal purpose. The Eternal Spirit alone can do that kind of an eternal work.

Perhaps we need an illustration here. Accomplished artists give their hands and eyes credit for their paintings. Musicians give their hands and fingers credit for the harmonies produced from keys or strings. Talented people everywhere think that their feet or hands or ears or vocal chords are the means of their productions. There never was a greater mistake than to believe that!

Give credit to the brain

The credit has to go to the marvelous brain that God has given every person. The hands have never really done anything except at the bidding and control of the brain. If the brain should suddenly be cut off and die, the hands will lie limp and helpless. It is the brain of a person that paints a picture, smells a rose, hears the sound of music.

This is all a matter of common physiology. All of us learned this fact in school, and doctors know it well in an advanced way. Your hand does not originate anything. If you crochet or paint, cut or trim, operate a machine—the origination and control rests with the brain, and the hands function only as the instruments through which the brain works.

The Holy Spirit must be to the members of the body of Christ what the brain is to eyes and ears and mouth and hands and fingers and feet. The Bible *does* say, "It is God who works in you to will and to act according to his good purpose" (Philippians 2:13). Someone may give me credit for something he or she thinks I have done for God. But in actuality, God is doing it and using me as an instrument, for there is a sense in which I am unable to do any spiritual work of any kind.

The important thing is that the Holy Spirit desires to take us and control us and use us as instruments and organs through whom He can express Himself in the body of Christ. Perhaps I can use my hands as a further illustration of this truth.

My hands are about average, I suppose—perhaps a little large for the size of my body, probably because I had to do a lot of farm work when I was a boy. But there is something I must tell you about these hands. They cannot play a violin. They cannot play the organ or the piano. They cannot paint a picture. They can barely hold a screwdriver to do a small repair job to keep things from falling apart at home. *I have ungifted hands.*

I am perfectly willing to paint a picture or play the organ, but my hands are ungifted. My brain can give some direction to these members of my body, but there is no response from my brain in the matter of form and coordination and perspective. If my brain should say, "Tozer, play something for us on the organ," I could only respond, "Brain, I would love to, but my hands know nothing of that gift!"

Let us be consistent

You will agree that it would be foolish for me to

try to bring forth any delightful organ music using such ungifted hands. Is it not appalling, then, to think that we allow this very thing to happen in the body of Christ? We enlist people and tell them to get busy doing God's work, failing to realize the necessity of the Spirit's control and functioning if there is to be a spiritual result.

Work that is only religious work and religious activity can be done by ungifted men and women, and it can be done within the framework of the Christian church. But it will wind up with this judgment upon it: It is only a product of a human mind.

Religious "activists" have many things of which they can boast. They build churches. They write hymns and books. Musically, they sing and play. Some of them will take time to engage in prayer. Others will organize movements and crusades and campaigns. But no matter how early in the morning they begin and no matter how late at night they stay with their projects, if it is an exercise of human talent for religious purposes, it can only wind up as a mortal brain doing a mortal job. And across it God will write a superscription: "It came to die, and it came to go!"

In our world today, mortality and temporality are written all across the church of Christ. The reason? So many persons are trying to do with human genius and in the power of the flesh what only God can do through the power of His Holy Spirit.

We must not be fooled by the loose and careless use of the word *immortal*. Art galleries claim that the paintings of Michelangelo are immortal. People of letters speak of the poetry of Elizabeth Browning as immortal. In truth, there are no immortal paintings, no immortal sonnets, no immortal musical compositions. Immortality is unending existence. I would rather be among those who are unknown, unsung and unheralded doing something through the Spirit of God that will count even a tiny little bit in the kingdom of God than to be involved in some highly-recognized expression of religious activity across which God will ultimately write the judgment: "This too shall pass!"

It is true that much church activity is thrown back upon a shaky foundation of psychology and natural talents. It is sad but true that many a mother-in-law is actually praying that her handsome son-in-law may be called to preach because "he would have such a marvelous pulpit presence."

We need discernment

We live in a day when charm is supposed to cover almost the entire multitude of sins. Charm has taken a great place in religious expression. I am convinced that our Lord expects us to be tough enough and cynical enough to recognize all of this that pleases the unthinking in our churches: the charm stuff, the stage presence in the pulpit, the golden qualities of voice.

We had better not forget what the apostle Paul said about "presence" and "speech." We recognize the fact that Paul was one of the greatest men who ever lived and that he became available as a human channel for a great work by God Almighty. But do you remember what they said about him in his day? The cosmopolitan Corinthians commented that " 'his letters are weighty and forceful, but in person he is unimpressive and his speaking amounts to nothing' " (2 Corinthians 10:10). When they read his first letter, they said, "He writes tremendous letters. This is great!" But later when they heard him in person, they were disappointed. He seemed to have so few natural talents.

Let us not miss the significance of that assessment. He had one of the world's greatest minds, but apparently he would have flunked any test given radio announcers. He had no charming pulpit presence. He had no golden qualities of voice or manner. But wherever he went he was led by the Holy Spirit. Whatever he did was at the prompting of the Holy Spirit. His great missionary work advanced the cause of Christ throughout the known world of his day.

I feel sorry for the church that decides to call a pastor because "his personality simply sparkles!" I have watched quite a few of those sparklers through the years. In reality, as every kid knows at Fourth of July time, sparklers can be an excitement in the neighborhood—but only for about one minute! Then you are left holding a hot stick that quickly cools off in your hand.

Many with sparkling personalities have come into our churches, but most of them have done their sparkling and are gone. The Holy Spirit rules out all of this sparkle and charm and pulpit presence and personal magnetism. Instead, He whispers to us: "God wants to humble you and fill you with Himself and control you so that you can become part of the eternal work that He wants to do in the earth in your day!"

A word of encouragement

Now, a word of encouragement. Just because the true gifts of the Spirit are so rare among us does not mean that they are missing entirely. There has never been a time in the history of the Christian church that some of the gifts were not present and effective. Sometimes they have functioned even among those who did not understand—or perhaps did not believe—in the same way that we think Christians should understand and believe. But the churches have prevailed and the faithful have been true to Christ. Link upon link, a chain of spiritual Christianity has been fashioned by the Holy Spirit.

What we do for God must be done in the power of the Holy Spirit. We know that we may have little praise from men. But what we do accomplish for Him as true spiritual work done with eternity in view will have His commendation written across it.

Most of us have never heard—or do not remember—the name of the humble 16-year-old girl whose singing brought such spiritual results in the Welsh revival with Evan Roberts. This quiet, humble girl would sing the gospel songs even though the singing of solos was not regularly a part of Welsh services. The Welsh sang in choral groups and used the metric psalter, which did not particularly lend itself to solo expression.

Considerable has been said and written about the young woman's spiritual gift—the Spirit-given ability to glorify the Savior when she would rise to sing. Not too much has been said about her voice. I do not know how much lyrical beauty or quality was in her voice, but the record is clear that she was a Spirit-gifted person. The Holy Spirit seemed to be singing and moving through her yielded expression.

When this girl sang about the Lord Jesus Christ and the plan of salvation, about the goodness and mercy of God and the need of all for the Savior, the Spirit brought His conviction and the hearts of men and women in the audience melted. Evan Roberts would rise to preach, and there was little left for him to do. He said that he would quote from the Scriptures and add an exhortation, and the people were ready to come to Jesus Christ. The soloist had melted them with the warmth and power of the Spirit. She humbly exercised the unusual gift that God had bestowed.

If she were singing today

Oh, what we would be tempted to do with her ministry in this day! We would put her on television and show off her talent—and spoil her. Thank God they knew better than to start writing her life story. Thank God she was not pressed into writing a book: *My Life: From Nursery to Platform!*

The girl was a beautiful example of what I have been pleading for: the humble use of our spiritual gifts for the glory of Jesus Christ. She was a simple Welsh girl willingly controlled by the Holy Spirit of God. As far as I know, there was never a music critic anywhere who said she had a good voice. But she had something far better. She had God's Spirit-given gift.

The Holy Spirit is the gentle Dove of God, and His coming to us in blessing and power is without pain or strain. The only painful part is the necessity of our own preparation, for the Holy Spirit will search us out completely and deal with us solemnly. He will guide us in necessary confessions that we must make. He will guide us in the necessity of ridding our lives of all that is selfish and unlike Jesus. He will guide us in getting straightened out with people with whom we have had differences. He will guide us in seeking forgiveness where it is necessary, and, in our willingness to be clean vessels, He will show us the necessity of old-fashioned restitution.

Some people who carry their big Bibles to impress others will never be filled with the Holy Spirit until they drop their sleek, smooth exterior of being "well taught" and earnestly desire God's humble plan for their lives. And after the desire must come a determination to go through with God on His terms. And even then, they will not be filled, owned and controlled by the Spirit of God until in desperation they throw themselves into the arms of God.

How about you? In the desire of your faith, have you closed your eyes and made the leap into the arms of Jesus? After all the help and instruction and study, after all the Bible verses you can remember have not done it, after every trick and everything you know to move toward God has failed, are you ready to cry to God from your heart, "Fill me now! Oh, fill me now!"

If so, you will move into that zone of obscurity where human reason has to be suspended for a moment and your heart leaps into the arms of God. It is at that point where human talent, human glory, human duty, human favor all flow out into the darkness of yesterday. Suddenly, everything is God's glory, God's honor, God's beauty, God's Spirit in your heart! You have been broken and melted and finally filled with His mighty Spirit to such a degree that no one can change your mind!

A personal testimony

I was 19 years old, earnestly in prayer, kneeling in the front room of my mother-in-law's home when I was baptized with a mighty infusion of the Holy Spirit. I had been eager for God's will, and I had been up against almost all of the groups and "isms" with their formulas and theories and teachings. They had tried to beat me down. Some said I went too far; others, that I had not gone far enough. But let me assure you that I know what God did for me and within me at that moment. Nothing on the outside held any important meaning. In desperation and in faith I took the leap away from everything that was unimportant to that which was most important: to be possessed by the Spirit of the Living God.

Any tiny work that God has ever done through me and through my ministry for Him dates back to that hour when I was filled with the Spirit. That is why I plead for the spiritual life of the body of Christ and the eternal ministries of the Eternal Spirit through God's children, His instruments.

CHAPTER

4

No Second-Class Christians: The Church Is Still the Church

The body is a unit, though it is made up of many parts; and though all its parts are many, they form one body. So it is with Christ. For we were all baptized by one Spirit into one body. . . .

Now you are the body of Christ, and each one of you is a part of it. (1 Corinthians 12:12–13, 27)

GOD PERPETUATES HIS CHURCH BY DOING in individual lives, generation after generation, what He did at Pentecost. Those who are truly Christians today are not in any way inferior to those who were truly Christians then. Such are the eternal promises of Jesus Christ to God's believing people.

Do we believe as truth and claim it as we should that the true church as it meets in the Name to worship the Presence finds Christ still giving Himself in the life of the fellowship? It is not the form that makes the church or its service. The Presence and the Name—these make the church. Wherever people are gathered together in the Name, there also is the Presence. The Presence and the Name constitute the true assembly of believers.

This brings to light a most wonderful truth. In the body of Christ there are no insignificant congregations. Each has His Name and each is honored by His Presence.

A young pastor, when introduced to a well-known church leader, commented, "Doctor, I am sure you don't know me. I am the pastor of just a little rural church."

The churchman wisely replied, "Young man, there are no little churches; all churches are the same size in God's sight."

Large or small, the church must be an assembly of believers brought together through a Name to worship a Presence. The blessed thing is that God does not ask whether it is a big church or a little church.

But people do insist on asking questions about size and number of people because they are carnal. I know all about such human judgments. "This is a very little church," or, "That is a poor, unknown church." Meanwhile, God is saying, "It is My church—they are all My churches, and each has every right to all I bestow!"

Every local church should be fully aware of its relationship to the church in the New Testament. We should ask ourselves if we are as truly interested in spiritual attainment as were the New Testament believers. We must confess that the spiritual temperature among us may often be lower than in the early church. But we cannot escape the message that those who truly meet in Jesus' Name to honor His Presence are included in a relationship that goes back to the New Testament and the apostles.

God perpetuates by repetition. Consider seriously with me some thoughts relating to that fact.

First, let us review how God perpetuates the human race. In every human being there is the mysterious and sacred life stream which God created in Adam and Eve. This has been perpetuated throughout the centuries by constant repetition in each generation. It is the same human race with the same human nature. Humanity simply repeats itself generation after generation.

You and I may not be the same as Adam or as Adam's grandchildren or great-great-great grandchildren. Nevertheless, we are as truly related to him as were his sons, Cain and Abel. Each of us is related to him by the mystery of procreation and the continuity of life that solidifies and holds together as one the whole human race.

It is true that we who inhabit the earth today are not the same persons who inhabited the earth when Columbus discovered America. Not one individual living now was alive then. Nevertheless, it is the same race. God has achieved the continuity of the human race by repeating each generation through the mystery of procreation.

The illustration of Israel

Israel is an illustration of this concept. The Israel of Moses' time was not the same Israel that basked in David's glory. It was, however, the same Israel by the repetition of procreation. It was the same God, the same covenant, the same relationship, the same revelation, the same fathers, the same intention and purpose. It was the same nation.

That is why God could speak to Israel in Moses'

day, in David's day and in Christ's day and be
speaking to the same Israel. Actually, it was the
same Israel secured and perpetuated in unbroken
continuity by the mystery of procreation and repetition.

So it is with the church of our Lord Jesus Christ—
the true church that is alive today. (In this context I
am not referring to lifeless, unbelieving churches. I
have in mind the true churches, the assemblies of
faithful believers.) We are not the same people who
made up the church in the days when Wesley
preached. And when Wesley preached, there was
not one person who was alive when Luther
preached. And when Luther preached, there was
not a man or woman remaining of those who lived
when Bernard, the ancient saint, wrote his great
hymns. My point is that each generation is a different group of people, but it is the same church that
comes down in unbroken lineal descent from the
earliest church.

This same continuity is not found in the progres-
sion of most national life. Nations have political
cohesion. The British Empire existed through its
many generations by means of political unity. But
political unity is not biological unity. The human
race, a unity by biological procreation, has a single
life stream, regardless of how people are broken up
into political distinctions.

And so it is with the church of Christ. It has
never been the political organization or segmenta-
tion that holds it together. When we talk about our
Protestant tradition—the tradition of the fathers—
we talk metaphorically and beautifully. But we do
not mean the same thing that I mean when I say

that a local assembly of faithful believers is in the lineage of the apostles. That is neither political nor ideological. It has to do with the mystery of life — with the life of God in man. The Holy Spirit does in the lives of people today what He did in the lives of the apostles and those first-century believers.

I appreciate and thank God for all the great and godly stalwarts in the history of the church. We regard them as leaders — though in reality they were servants, even as you and I are. Luther sowed, Wesley watered, Finney reaped. They were servants of the living God. And though we respect people like these, we actually follow none of them. Our charter goes farther back and is from a higher source.

We are part of the church founded by the Lord Jesus Christ and perpetuated by the mystery of the new birth. Therefore our assembly is that of Christian believers gathered under a Name to worship and adore a Presence.

If this is true — and everything within me witnesses that it is — all the strain is gone. Even the strain about traditional religious forms is gone. The pressures to sing certain songs, recite certain prayers and creeds, follow accepted liturgies, conform to traditional patterns of ministerial leadership — all of these pale in importance as we function in faith as God's people who glorify the Name above every name and honor His Presence!

Yes, I contend that God is able to do for us today all that He did in the days of the apostles. Oh, the power that is ours — the potential we possess because He is here! Our franchise still stands. There has been no revocation of our charter!

If a poll should be taken today to name the 10 greatest men in the world and our names were not included, we would still have the same privileges in God's world that they would have. We can breathe God's beautiful air, look at His blue sky, gaze into a never-ending array of stars in the night sky. We can stand upon the hard earth and stamp our feet and know that it will sustain us. We are as much a part of this human race as the greatest men and women.

And spiritually there is no blessing or privilege ever given by God that is withheld from us today— understanding, of course, that we know what the Bible really says. For instance, we know that we cannot have the new heavens and the new earth right now—although we can have the essence of them in our beings now. We also know that right now we cannot have the new body that God is going to give at the coming of Christ. But all things that are for us now we can have, and it is easy to find out what they are.

Why is it?

Why is it, then, that believers are not experiencing all that God desires for them? Why is it that our church attendance has become a social thing? Why does church and Christianity become merely form and ritual?

It is because we are badly instructed. We have been badly taught. We have been told that we are different now, and have been ever since the passing of the apostles. We are advised, "This is a different age in the church. The devil is busy and we cannot have or know what the apostolic church had and knew."

I react strongly to that kind of teaching. Any person who dares to say such things is in the same position as a man who refuses to let *your* children open *your* pantry door or sit down at *your* table and eat. Any kind of teaching or exposition, so called, that shuts you out of the privileges and promises of the New Testament is wrong, and the person who tries to shut you out is a false teacher!

Who gave anyone the right to stand at your dining room table at mealtime and not let your children partake of the food? Who has the right, in the name of bad teaching, to keep your children from your table? They are your children and you are responsible for them. You have an unwritten covenant with them, and that table is spread for them. You may reserve the right to tell them how they should behave, but you do not have the right to shut them out.

I ask, then, what right has any person to tell me, in the name of Bible teaching, that I belong to a different church from the first-century, apostolic church? Who is authorized to tell me that the fire has dimmed down in glory and the mighty arm of God's Christ is now a diminished power? When I read the New Testament, who has been commissioned to say, "But this part is not for you. That portion is not for you. That promise is not for you?" Who has been given the right to stand thus at the door to the kingdom of God?

No one!

Any kind of teaching or Bible exposition that shuts me out from the privileges and promises of the New Testament is wrong. The person who tries to so deprive me is a false teacher.

Another reason why we do not receive as much from God as we should is because of the general low level of spiritual enthusiasm and the chilling effect of bad example. We would be foolish to try to deny either one.

I hope you will never go into panic when some cynic announces, "I repudiate the Christian church because of all the bad things I know about certain congregations!" There are always pretenders. You and I have heard of instances of fleshly extravagance among professing followers of Christ. It cannot be denied that such behavior is always a hindrance to the faith—and discourages faithfulness on the part of others.

Now, bad examples are one thing, but would we repudiate the 12 apostles because there was a Judas? Or the thousands of devoted believers in Jerusalem because there were an Ananias and a Sapphira? Would we repudiate Paul because there was a Demas? Certainly not!

And I refuse to repudiate the assembly of the saints just because a bad example turns up occasionally. I doubt that any one of us following the Lord has been so perfect that he or she could claim never to have been a bad example. But forgiveness and restoration are part of what our Christian gospel and the victorious life in the body of Christ is all about! It is the blood of the everlasting covenant that makes the sinner clean and makes the weak strong, providing forgiveness and justification through God's mercy and grace.

What God has made clean let us never call unclean. There is a fountain filled with blood, and whatever the past life of the child of God, his or her present life is revealed by the Spirit as a beautiful gift from God witnessing to the Savior in the fellowship of the body.

Christ sealed that eternal covenant of grace with His blood when He gave Himself on the cross. It is a covenant that cannot be broken. It is a covenant that has never been amended or edited.

The power and the provisions, the promises and the gifts that marked the early church can belong to us now. If we will let Him, Christ will do in us and through us that which He did in and through the committed believers right after Pentecost.

The potential is ours. Do we dare believe that the faithful Christian believers may yet experience a great new wave of spiritual power? It probably will not happen across the wide, broad church with its amusements and worldly nonsense, but it will surely come to those who desire the presence and blessing of God more than they want anything else. It will come to the humble, faithful, devoted believers, whoever and wherever they are.

To miss out in any degree on all that God provides for us is tragedy—pure and simple. No Christian can afford to miss God's best. I confess I want to be in such a spiritual condition that I may share in God's blessings as they come, no matter what the cost may be.

And I want you, as a follower of Christ and in lineal descent from the apostles, when you meet with fellow believers in the Name to honor the Presence, to share, too, in all His fullness.

5

An Assembly of Saints: Unity in the Spirit

God has arranged the parts in the body, every one of them, just as he wanted them to be. . . .

God has combined the members of the body and has given greater honor to the parts that lacked it, so that there should be no division in the body. . . .

Now you are the body of Christ, and each one of you is a part of it. (1 Corinthians 12:18, 24–25, 27)

THE CHRISTIAN CHURCH IS THE ASSEMBLY of redeemed saints. That is stating it as basically as possible. And in what is probably the most fundamental teaching in the New Testament concerning Christ and His church, Paul relates the life and service of the church to a unity which can only be wrought by the Holy Spirit.

Paul specifically reminded the first century Corinthian believers that "the body is a unit, though it is made up of many parts; and though all its parts are many, they form one body." Then he added, "So it is with Christ. For we were all baptized by one Spirit into one body—whether Jews or Greeks, slave or free—and we were all given the one Spirit to drink" (1 Corinthians 12:12–13).

Now in our local church or assembly, we realize

we are not an end in ourselves. If we are going to be what we ought to be in the local church, we must come to think of ourselves as a part of something much more expansive, something that encompasses our entire world. We need to see the church, the body of Christ, as a whole.

There is an important sense here in which we discover that we "belong." We belong to something that God has brought into being, something that is worthy and valuable, something that is going to last forever. You and I do not have to be ashamed for wanting to belong to the work that God is doing through His church.

People need to "belong"

Sociologists and psychologists talk about the need for belonging. They tell us that a rejected child, one who no longer belongs to anyone, will develop dangerous mental and nervous traits. Those neighborhood youth gangs that roam and terrorize our inner cities come largely from homes where they have been rejected. Many young children of the ghettos cannot recall ever being loved by a mother or a father. So they find some answer to their own inner need by belonging to a gang. In their "belonging" to others, these youths have found a new sense of human strength and worth, however misdirected it may be.

So it is with people in every walk of life. The same longing is behind the popularity of the secret orders and societies. Men who are pushed around by their wives or submerged and humiliated by their superiors at work soon get the feeling that they have no soul to call their own. Because they need some point where they can rally their self-respect, they join a lodge or fraternal society. They "belong" to something.

Perhaps you saw the cartoon in which the wife was blocking the doorway of the house while saying to her husband: "The high exalted potentate can't go out tonight because I won't let him!"

Joining is not necessarily a bad thing. We humans are by nature gregarious. We are not wolves, who go alone or travel in small packs that quickly break up. We are sheep. Sheep travel together in flocks and stay together for a lifetime.

But our concern right now is the church, the body of Christ. You may be—probably are—a member of a local congregation, but you also have the joyful sense of belonging to an amazing fellowship of the redeemed throughout the world! This is entirely different from belonging to a man-made order or society or group.

My American upbringing has made my knees hard to bend—unless God bends them. I cannot imagine myself getting down on my knees and swearing allegiance to some order of this or some secret society of that. But I am not ashamed that I want to belong to something good and great and eternal—the church of Jesus Christ.

By nature we are gregarious

No person in his or her right mind wants to go it alone. The hermit, who lives alone in his attic, refusing to answer the door, sneaking out in the dark to secure a little food—that man is sick. He is not normal. A normal person wants to walk outside, look around at others of his kind, and reflect:

"I belong! This is my race. These are my people. They are speaking my language. That is my flag there on top of the school building. I belong here!" Those feelings are necessary to our human well-being—to our physical and mental health. And that is why unwanted children and others who feel rejected may develop serious and even dangerous behavioral traits.

As Christians, we enjoy singing songs about the church because we have come to think of ourselves in relation to the whole church of Christ. Our hymns repeat with meaning that we are the church universal, the whole body of the redeemed. Jesus Christ purchased us with His own blood. We are the church, part now in heaven and part on earth. We are "from every nation, tribe, people and language" (Revelation 7:9). I am thankful to be a part of that body that transcends denominations, orders, political boundaries and every other man-made division.

But this church encompasses not just the true believers of our present day but believers all the way back to Pentecost. I believe in a true apostolic succession. I do not refer to a succession of bishops—men with names and organizations—but to the perpetuation of that true church of Christ that began at Pentecost. There the Holy Spirit came upon a body of believers and made them one. They became God's people in a sense that none of them had ever been before.

This is an important biblical concept. Every believing Christian down through the centuries has a part with us and we have a part with every faithful Christian group throughout the world. We are one!

When I hear of some good things said or done by a Christian, wherever he or she may be on our earth, I have a warm feeling in my heart. That word or that act has become a part of me—it belongs to me, and I am a part of it. No matter that I may never personally meet the person in this world. The church of our Lord is one.

But even more important than our relationship with believers worldwide and through the centuries is our relationship with the Head of the church, Jesus Christ.

First things first

A Chicago minister got his name in the papers by his efforts to persuade all the members of his congregation to vote. Now good Christian citizens should vote, but that is each person's private business. I do not intend to needle non-voters—except to remind them that, by and large, we get the kind of leaders we deserve. I am much more deeply concerned about people's relationships to God and about believers' continuing spiritual lives. Before there were Democrats and Republicans, or Tories and Whigs, or Socialists and Christian Fronts, there was God. And before men and women ever knew the privilege of the ballot, there was God.

There is no doubt in my mind that a person's relationship to God must come first—absolutely! After that comes his or her relationship to others, followed by such matters as service for our Lord and habits of life.

What about corporate prayer? It is a high Christian privilege to pray for one another within each local church body and then for other believers throughout the world. As a Christian minister, I have no right to preach to people I have not prayed for. That is my strong conviction.

Some like to shy away from the word *duty*. But I have a duty to pray for those who are striving to walk with God in the fellowship of the church. A frisky young colt in the pasture knows nothing about duty. But that colt's well-trained, hard-working mother in the harness pulling a wagon or a plow is well acquainted with duty. The colt only knows freedom; the work horse knows duty.

I cannot help but wonder if our inordinate desire for freedom and our strange fear of duty have had an effect upon the life of the church. People ought to consider it a privilege as well as a sacred duty to pray for their church and for others who are included in the fellowship of the Christian faith.

I know there are those who attend churches where there is never any appeal or desire to engage in effectual prayer for others. Church members can recite the name of their church, the date it was organized and what part it plays in the "religious community." But that is not enough. Strictly speaking, no one can bring a true segment of the body of Christ into being simply through organization.

Organization is not wrong

I do not want to be misunderstood. Within our Christian fellowships and in our efforts to evangelize, there must of necessity be some proper organization. Paul wrote to Titus and told him to set things in order and to appoint men to tasks within each fellowship. So organization has scriptural precedent. But you cannot organize a Christian church in the same way you would organize a baseball club. In baseball you need a captain, a certain number of pitchers, catchers, infielders, outfielders and coaches. And whether or not the club wins any games, it is an organized ball club.

But a Christian church cannot be organized in that sense. Even after the adoption of a proper church constitution there may not actually be a New Testament church. Perhaps the New Testament church is within that organization, but that organization is not the church, for the church is the assembly of the saints.

No church congregation has the right to feel that it has finally arrived and is fully matured. Every congregation with a true desire for the knowledge of God must continually be reaching out—determining its own needs and what it should be in order to please the Lord. It must continue in the study of the Bible to determine what the Holy Spirit wants to do in the life of the organic church and how the Spirit will provide the power and special abilities to glorify Jesus Christ.

To accomplish all this requires in itself a gift of the Spirit! Note the words of Isaiah:

> A shoot will come up from the stump of Jesse;
> from his roots a Branch will bear fruit.
> The Spirit of the Lord will rest on him—
>   The Spirit of wisdom and of understanding,
>   the Spirit of counsel and of power,
>   the Spirit of knowledge and of the fear of the
>   Lord—
> and he will delight in the fear of the Lord.

He will not judge by what he sees with his
    eyes,
or decide by what he hears with his ears;
but with righteousness he will judge the needy,
    with justice he will give decisions for the
    poor of the earth. . . .
Righteousness will be his belt
    and faithfulness the sash around his waist.
    (11:1-5)

All of that was spoken by the prophet concerning
Jesus, the One who was to come to Israel. But
should not that description of spiritual life and
ministry also be true of all who by faith are members of the body of Christ?

From Head to feet

In the Old Testament, when the oil of anointing
was poured on the high priest's head, it ran down
to the skirt of his garment and onto his feet, giving
fragrance and sweetness to his whole body. So the
mighty power that was poured upon Jesus as Head
of the church must flow down to every member of
His body. What was true of Jesus, our Lord, should
be just as true of those, clergy and lay people, who
minister His grace and truth.

The Spirit of wisdom and of understanding,
    the Spirit of counsel and of power,
    the Spirit of knowledge and of the fear of the
    Lord—
and he will delight in the fear of the Lord.

What a powerful message from the prophet to
our own day!

He will not judge by what he sees with his
eyes.

The curse of modern Christian leaders is their
propensity to look around and take their spiritual
bearings from what they see, rather than from what
the Lord has said.

. . . or decide by what he hears with his ears.

Is this not what we are prone to do in church
leadership? Do we not listen to learn which way
others are moving and then act accordingly? But
the Spirit of God never leads us into that mistake.

With righteousness he will judge the needy,
    with justice he will give decisions for the
        poor of the earth. . . .
Righteousness will be his belt
    and faithfulness the sash around his waist.

Led by the Spirit of God, the members of the
body of Christ will always be right in spirit, right in
their wisdom, right in their judgment. They will
not be judged—they will not allow themselves to
be judged—on the basis of what is currently taking
place all around them.

God wants to do a new thing

God wants to do something new and blessed for
every believer who has the inner desire to know
Him better. I know it takes a store of patience and
persistence and much courage to find and pursue
the will of God in this day. Of late there has been
revival in many churches. I see no reason why it

should not flow out and down—and over and up and around—until we are all swimming in it!

In our local church assemblies we mingle with each other, we worship the Lord Christ. We confess that all of the privileges and responsibilities rest upon us that once rested upon those believers at Pentecost. The plan and promises of God for His believing children have not diminished one little bit. Nowhere in the Word of God is there any text that can be twisted into teaching that the organic living church of Jesus Christ just prior to His return will not have every right, every power, every obligation that she had at Pentecost.

I for one am determined that we will not capitulate to the times in which we live! There is such a thing as just getting tough about this. In the power of the Spirit we must say, "I am not yielding and I will not yield to the time in which I live!" We can say that to our Lord, to ourselves and, betimes, maybe, over our shoulders to the devil!

The faithful body of Christ will not give up to the ways of the world or even to the more common ways of religion that are all about us. Faithful believers will not succumb to the temptation to judge themselves by what others are doing. Neither will they allow their assemblies to be judged, or their spiritual body life affected, by the attitudes of others. They will be happy and continue to rejoice in the fact that they have taken the New Testament standard as their standard.

It is not sufficient for a local church simply to have the label of orthodoxy. All of us who love our Lord Jesus Christ face great changes in this period before His return. We must re-experience the kind of spiritual revival that will eventuate in new moral power, a new willingness to separate from the world, a new heart purity, a new bestowal of the gifts of the Holy Spirit of God.

The alternative: abandonment

If we are unwilling for this, I believe that God will somehow raise up others to carry the torch. If we do not make a hard-rudder return to the very roots of our Christian faith, Christian teaching and Christian living, God is going to pass us up! He will pass us up as a farmer deals with egg shells that are empty. He carries them out and buries them, just as we bury the dead after the human spirit has departed.

There was a day when leaders in Israel, believing in the perpetuity of their nation's place in the sun, boasted to Jesus, "We are Abraham's descendants and have never been slaves of anyone" (John 8:33). They said, "The only Father we have is God" (8:41). But Jesus replied that Abraham's true descendants were those who did the works of Abraham (8:39), that *their* father was not Abraham, but the devil (8:44).

The Jewish leaders looked proudly at their beautiful, massive temple and said to Jesus, "It has taken forty-six years to build this temple" (2:20). But Jesus predicted a coming day when not one stone would be left atop another (Matthew 24:2). That, of course, came to pass when the Roman emperor sent his legions against Jerusalem. He had never heard those prophetic words of Jesus, but he was the means of their fulfillment in the program of God. It had been a sacred temple to the Jews, but the Roman conquerors knocked down every stone level with the ground.

God can deal ruthlessly with nations and men and men's favorite religions and temples. There is no religious group or church organization in the world that God will not abandon if it ceases to fulfill His divine will. Ecclesiastical robes are not impressive enough or gold crosses heavy enough or titles long enough to save the church once she ceases to fulfill the will of God among sinful men who need the transforming news of Christ's gospel.

The God who raised them up in centuries past will turn away unless they continue to fulfill the gracious will of God, following on to know the Lord, walking humbly and meekly in faith and love. Crowds do not impress the Almighty. Size is not a significant matter with Him. He will turn His blessing to some small mission, to a simple-hearted people somewhere whose greatest possession is the desire to love Him and obey Him.

I am speaking here about organizations, not the individual members. God never leaves or forsakes His believing children. But I surely believe that God has lifted the cloud and the fire of His presence from churches that forsook Him and His eternal Word.

We may lack everything else, but we must have the cloud and the fire of God's presence. We must have the enabling and the power of the Holy Spirit. We must have the glow of the Shekinah glory— God with us. Then, even lacking all else, we still will have a true church!

6

God's Eternal Purpose: Christ, Center of All Things

While they were still talking about this, Jesus himself stood among them and said to them, "Peace be with you." (Luke 24:36)

CONTRARY TO THE OPINION OF MANY, Christianity was never intended to be an "ethical system" headed by Jesus Christ. Our Lord did not come to earth to launch a new religious system. He came to be our religion—if I dare put it that way. He came with eternal purpose. He came to be the center of all things.

Jesus came in person—enfleshed—to be God's salvation to the very ends of the earth. He did not come simply to delegate power to others to heal or to bless. He came to *be* the blessing, for all blessing and God's full glory are to be found in Him.

Because Jesus Christ is the center of all things, He offers deliverance to us by His direct, personal touch. This is not a one-man interpretation on my part. It is the basic teaching of salvation through the Messiah-Savior. It runs throughout the Bible.

Jesus Christ came into a world religiously complex. We might liken it to a religious jungle. Just within the borders of His own nation, people were burdened with a choking and confusing multiplicity of duties, rituals and observances. In Israel alone, it was a dark jungle grown thick with manmade rules.

Into that darkness came the true Light that gives light to everyone. Because He shone so brightly, dispelling the darkness, He could say and teach, "I am the light of the world" (John 8:12). He came in the fullness of time to be God's salvation — God's cure for all that was wrong with the human race. He came to deliver us from our moral and spiritual disorders — and from our own failed remedies.

Religion is one of the heaviest burdens that has ever been laid upon the human race. People have been forever using it as a kind of self-medication. Conscious of their own moral and spiritual disorders, they try a dose of religion, hoping to get better by their own treatment.

Mankind has tried everything

I often wonder if there is any kind of self-cure or human medication that people have not tried in their efforts to restore themselves and gain merit. In India, millions of pilgrims may be seen prostrate on the ground, crawling like inchworms toward the Ganges River, hoping that a dip in the sacred waters will release them from the burden of guilt.

Countless numbers have tried to deal with guilt by abstaining from food and drink and by other forms of self-denial. People have tortured themselves, wearing hair shirts, walking on spikes, running over hot coals. Others have shunned society —

hiding in caves, living in monasteries—hoping to gain some merit that would compensate for their sinful natures and bring them closer to God. Even in our own day and in our own land, the attempts at self-medication still go on. People fail to recognize that the Cure for what ails them has already come.

Simeon, the old man of God who had waited a life-time for the Messiah, knew that the Cure had come! When he saw Joseph and Mary and the baby Jesus in the temple courts, he took Jesus in his arms and exclaimed,

> Sovereign, Lord, as you have promised,
>   you now dismiss your servant in peace.
> For my eyes have seen your salvation,
>   which you have prepared in the sight of all
>   people,
> a light for revelation to the Gentiles
>   and glory to your people Israel.
> (Luke 2:29-30)

So, I repeat, it is Jesus Christ Himself whom Christianity offers. And He is enough! A person's relation to Jesus Christ is the all-important matter in this life. And that fact is both good news and bad. It is good news for all who have met the Savior and know Him intimately and personally. It is bad news for those who hope to get to heaven some other way.

In the Bible text with which this chapter began, Jesus is saying to His followers, "Peace be with you." He spoke those words to His 11 remaining disciples "and those with them" the evening of His resurrection. The two followers who had been joined by Jesus on the road to Emmaus had returned to the company of disciples in Jerusalem to report the joyous revelation. Before they could open their mouths, those in Jerusalem were volunteering their own glad announcement: "It is true! The Lord has risen and has appeared to Simon" (Luke 24:34). While the Emmaus disciples and the Jerusalem disciples were exchanging experiences, "Jesus himself stood among them and said to them, 'Peace be with you.' "

Jesus is our peace

It is a beautiful explanation of the angels' words, "On earth peace to men on whom [God's] favor rests" (Luke 2:14). The angels could make such a declaration only because it was Jesus who had come. He is our peace. Because of Him, the angels could announce, "Peace on earth."

This portion of Scripture illustrates Jesus' method of imparting health, directly and personally. It was Christ in the midst—at the center—and He could take that place because He is God. He is spirit, timeless, spaceless, supreme. He is all and in all. Therefore, He could be at the center. He is the hub of the wheel—to borrow an ancient and well-used illustration—around which all else revolves. Centuries ago someone said that Christ is like the hub and everything that has been created is on the rim of the wheel. The statement reminds me of what one of the old church fathers said: "Everything that exists is equally distant from Jesus and equally near to Him." When Jesus Christ has His proper place as hub, we are all equally close or equally far from Him.

Jesus is in the midst, and because that is true, He is accessible from anywhere in life. This is good news, wonderful good news!

Jesus Christ is at the center of *geography*. No one, therefore, can claim an advantage with Christ because of location.

At the time of the historic Crusades, many believed they could gain merit by making a pilgrimage to the very places where Jesus had been during His time on earth, particularly to the sepulcher where His body had been laid.

When Peter the Hermit, old and barefooted, whipped all of Europe into a white heat to get the Crusades launched, he set the goal of liberating a grave out of which Jesus Christ had stepped more than a millennium before. The Crusaders felt that if that empty tomb could be taken from the Muslims, everything would be all right. Today people are still fascinated by the grave where Jesus supposedly lay.

He is not there!

Why are we so spiritually obtuse? Have we not heard Jesus' words? He said, "A time is coming when you will worship the Father neither on this mountain [in Samaria] nor in Jerusalem. . . . The true worshipers will worship the Father in spirit and truth, for they are the kind of worshipers the Father seeks. God is spirit, and his worshipers must worship in spirit and in truth" (John 4:21–24).

I wonder why the Crusaders did not consider that. Why all the starvation, the suffering, the blood? Why the long, weary treks to get to the place where Jesus was born, where He was crucified, where He died? There is no geographical advantage anywhere in the world. Not one of us will be a better Christian by living in Jerusalem. And not one of us is disadvantaged spiritually for living far from Judea or Galilee.

Jesus Christ is in the very center of geography. Every place is just as near to Him as every other place! And every place is just as far, also. Geography means nothing in our relationship to our Savior and Lord.

Great amounts of money have been spent by preachers who felt they could preach better if only they visited the Holy Land. So they have gone over to look on Jerusalem and Bethlehem and Nazareth and Capernaum. And when they come back, they merely have a few more stories to tell. Actually, they are morally no better and their audiences are morally no better. Let us believe it: Jesus is the hub, and geography is all around Him!

Not only is Christ the center of geography, but we must come to the conclusion that He is also the center of *time*. Many wish wistfully that they might have been living in Palestine when Jesus was on earth. In Sunday school we used to sing a song to that effect:

> I think when I read that sweet story of old,
>   When Jesus was here among men,
> How He called little children as lambs to His
>   fold,
>   I should like to have been with Him then.

Many a tear has been dabbed at by people singing that song. But did you know that those who were with Jesus at the time He walked Judea's mountains and Galilee's shores were not as well off as they were 10 days after He left them? Ten days after His ascension, He sent the Holy Spirit, and the disciples who understood only partially while they were with Jesus suddenly knew the plan of God as in a blaze of light.

Deliver us from short-sightedness!

Still people say, "I would like to have lived in the time of Christ." Why? There were hypocrites and Pharisees and opposers in the time of Christ. There were unbelievers and murderers. They would not have found things any better 2,000 years ago. Those who look back with nostalgia upon what they consider the good old days need to be delivered from such short-sightedness!

Consider, too, that Jesus Christ is the center of the *human race*. He does not favor one race above another. Jesus Christ is the Son of Man. He is not the Son of the Jewish race only. He is the Son of all races, no matter what the skin color or the spoken language. When He became incarnated in mortal flesh, it was not simply in the body of a Jew but in a body that fit the whole human race.

You can go to Tibet or Mongolia, you can go to the Indians of South America, the Muslims of Iran, the tribespeople of West Africa, the Scots of Glasgow and preach Jesus Christ. If there is faith and a willingness to follow, Jesus will bring them into His fellowship. They are all in the rim—equally far, equally near.

Christ is also at the center of all *cultural levels*. That is the reason my church, The Christian and Missionary Alliance, holds the missionary philosophy it does. Alliance missionaries do not first go into a country to educate the people and then preach Christ to them. They know better than that! They know that Jesus Christ is just as near to an unschooled Islander as He is to an erudite American or Britisher. Preach Christ and show the love of God to the most primitive, neglected people in the world. Be patient until the Holy Spirit gives them understanding. Their hearts will awaken. The Spirit will illuminate their minds. Those who come to faith in Jesus will be transformed. It is a beautiful thing to see, and it is being demonstrated over and over in the world today. In parts of Indonesia, for example, so-called stone age people only a generation removed from cannibalism, are being born again just as quickly as those with college degrees. It is just as near to Jesus from the jungle as it is from the ivy-covered halls.

The center of our years

Christ is also at the center of all our *human years* of life. It is just as near to Jesus for the 80-year-old as the eight-year-old; just as near for the 50-year-old as the five-year-old. Of course, we are told that as we get older we are harder to reach for God, and the likelihood of our turning to Christ diminishes. But our ability to come to Jesus—the distance we are from God—is no greater when we are 90 than when we were youngsters.

For the Christian, our Lord is in the center of all our experiences, ready to speak His benediction of peace. An experience is the awareness of things taking place around us. A newborn baby does not have experience because he or she does not have awareness. He or she is just a little stranger in our world. But that baby learns fast—beginning with the discovery that crying gets attention!

The man or woman who lives to be 100 has really had some experiences. But if the person has lived a lifetime in the hills, seldom coming out, he or she may have a narrow field of experience. Conversely, the well-educated world traveler with a wide circle of friends has experiences so vast that it is a mystery as to how his or her brain can file away so much for future memory and reference.

But I ask, who is nearer to Jesus? Does the child with little experience have an advantage over the person of wide experience? There is no difference! Jesus Christ stands in the middle of life's experiences, and anyone can reach Him, no matter who he or she is. Jonathan Edwards, that mighty 18th century New England preacher, was converted when he was only five years old. He wrote, "I never backslid. I went right on."

Consider the boy Samuel and the old priest, Eli. Samuel may have been 12. Eli was 98. What experiences had the boy had? Some, to be sure. But not compared with Eli's. Eli had run the whole scale, the gamut of human possibilities. Yet the distance to God was no different for young Samuel, with little experience, than for Eli, who had discovered through the years what life was all about.

When Jesus was crucified, you will remember, the superscription, "This is Jesus Christ, the King of the Jews," placed above His head was in three languages: Hebrew, Greek and Latin. Someone has pointed out that in sovereignly arranging that detail, God took in the whole world. Hebrew stands for religion, Greek for philosophy and Latin for

Rome's military prowess. All the possibilities of human experience on a world scale were wrapped up in those three languages.

No one had the advantage of closeness

It was just as close from the Roman soldiers to the Son of God as from the Hebrew teacher, Nicodemus, who said, "Rabbi, we know you are a teacher who has come from God" (John 3:2). And it was just as close for Dionysius and Damaris, the Athenian Greek intellectuals who believed after Paul addressed the meeting of the Areopagus (Acts 17:34).

Like the world of that day, we still have religion, culture-philosophy and the military-political. Everything seems to fall somewhere within those brackets. Jesus Christ was crucified in the very center of our human world. So it is just as easy to reach Him from the philosopher's ivory tower as from the priest's sanctuary. It is just as easy for the uniformed soldier or the political leader to reach Him as it is for the thinker amid his big books.

Jesus our Lord stands in the midst so no one can claim advantage. I thank God that no one can intimidate me or send me away from Him. No one can put me down, saying, "Ah, but you don't know." They have tried. They smile when they say it and I smile back and think, *You are the one who doesn't know—because I know!* I know I can reach Jesus as quickly from where I am as any other person.

Einstein, with his great mind, could have reached out and touched his Messiah if he would. There are many in American who can neither read or write. Einstein and the man or woman who makes an X for a signature are in the same category as far as Jesus is concerned. Both are equal on the rim. No one can truthfully say he or she has an advantage over someone else.

You ask, "If that is the case, why doesn't everybody reach out to Jesus?"

Because of inexcusable stubbornness.

Because of unbelief.

Because they are preoccupied with other things.

Because they do not really believe they need Him.

Millions turn their backs on Jesus Christ because they will not confess their need. If God the Holy Spirit has helped you realize your need, I have good news. You can go to Jesus Christ in faith. You can touch Him. You can feel His power flowing out to help you, whoever you are, whatever your station in life.

Jesus did not come to save learned people only. He came to save sinners. He did not come to save white people only. He came to save people whatever their skin color. He did not come to save children and youth only. He came to save people of all ages.

Jesus is in the midst—just as near to you as to anyone else. He wants to bless you with His peace. And the most important thing about you and Jesus is that you can reach Him from where you are!

7

The Failing Believer: God Has a Remedy

My dear children, I write this to you so that you will not sin. But if anybody does sin, we have one who speaks to the Father in our defense—Jesus Christ, the Righteous One. He is the atoning sacrifice for our sins, and not only for ours but also for the sins of the whole world. (1 John 2:1–2)

THERE IS CLEAR TEACHING THROUGHOUT the Old and New Testaments concerning God's willingness to forgive and forget our sins. But there are segments of the Christian church that appear to be poorly taught concerning God's remedy through the atonement for the believer who has yielded to temptation and failed his Lord.

It is important that we know how to both encourage and deal with the distressed and guilt-ridden disciple who cries out in utter dejection and misery of soul: "I quit! I quit! It is no use. I am just worse than other people!"

Just why does God forgive sin, anyway?

God forgives sin because He knows that sin is the dark shadow standing between Him and His highest creation, mankind. God is more willing to remove that shadow than we are to have it removed.

He *wants* to forgive us; that desire is a part of His character.

The Word of God gives me the blessed authority to announce that all of God's believing children have a remedy for the guilt of sin. "Bring your sacrifice! Bring your sacrifice!" the Old Testament urges.

In the Old Testament pattern of forgiveness, the Jew had to bring a female goat (Leviticus 4:28). In this church age, the New Testament Christian surely knows that he can bring no offering other than his trust in the eternal Lamb of God, offered once and forever efficacious.

John is not excusing sin

By no stretch of the imagination can anyone claim that the apostle John was excusing sin when he wrote this important first letter. Actually, his paragraphs bristle with condemnation of everything evil. They carry the message of a sin-hating God. But under the inspiration of the Holy Spirit, John takes the position of a realist and indicates what our Lord has done to make it possible for weak and vacillating believers to find forgiveness and assurance in their daily lives.

The apostle is not suggesting some theoretical posture for believers. He is not conjecturing on how things should be. He is taking things as he found them and dealing with them on the basis of their reality. John was a father in the Christian faith and had wide experience with human beings, particularly with redeemed human beings. With the Holy Spirit's guidance, this mature apostle advises Christian believers to be aware of their dependency on the Lord moment by moment. We can count on it: during our lives there will never be a time when at least the possibility of sinning is not present.

John's language cannot be interpreted as encouragement for those in the kingdom of God to sin carelessly or willfully. Rather, he points out a kind of spiritual clinic for the Christian who strays into trouble.

In our great manufacturing and industrial complexes, it is common to find clinics or infirmaries maintained by the companies for their employees. Are these companies thereby encouraging accidents and illnesses? No. But these companies can predict from industry-wide statistics approximately how many accidents and how much sickness there will be among their employees. Recognizing the human situation and being aware of the statistics, they realistically make provision for anticipated need.

So John is not offering an encouragement to sin. He is saying, in effect, "Watch out and do not sin. But *if* you sin, you have an Advocate with your Father God." That Advocate—that Representative— is Jesus Christ, the Righteous One. John continues by assuring us that Jesus is the atoning sacrifice for our sins. Then he adds a beautiful, expansive parenthesis: "Not only for [our sins] but also for the sins of the whole world."

In passing, I note that this "clinic" idea was actually instituted in Old Testament times. Go back to Leviticus 4 to connect the Old and New Testament plans of forgiveness. You will see that the same Holy Spirit provided the inspiration throughout the Bible. And the same eternal Christ shines through every page and every chapter.

God has provided a "clinic"

Leviticus 4 speaks of a spiritual "clinic" provided for the people of Israel who had become infected with evil and wrongdoing. Even in that period of Law, God offered an immediate and efficacious remedy for those who fell short of His commands. Notice what they were told to do about sin:

> When a member of the community sins unintentionally and does what is forbidden in any of the Lord's commands, he is guilty. When he is made aware of the sin he committed, he must bring as his offering for the sin he committed a female goat without defect. He is to lay his hand on the head of the sin offering and slaughter it at the place of the burnt offering. Then the priest is to take some of the blood with his finger and put it on the horns of the altar of burnt offering and pour out the rest of the blood at the base of the altar. He shall remove all the fat, just as the fat is removed from the fellowship offering, and the priest shall burn it on the altar as an aroma pleasing to the Lord. In this way the priest will make atonement for him, and he will be forgiven. (4:27–31)

First, note that some wrongs may be done through ignorance. The words *through ignorance* should not cause you to picture in your mind a starry-eyed, honest-hearted person who just happened to sin accidentally. Realistically we must face up to the fact that here is a careless person, one who perhaps has neglected the Scriptures and their warnings. He or she has followed the intent of his or her own deceptive heart and has sinned against the commandments of the Lord. But, thankfully, God is concerned! God has provided a remedy for that person's careless act of sin.

In Leviticus 4, God's remedy for sin and wrong-doing was provided for several categories of persons within Israel. Verse 3 speaks of "the anointed priest" who sins. I wish that did not have to be in the record—but I am glad it is. Those religious leaders were still human and imperfect.

The godly Saint Theresa confessed that she felt she was the least of all Christians because she read of Christ's great saints before her time who from the day of their conversion lived so earnestly for God that they no longer caused Him any grief by sinning. She wrote: "I cannot say that. I have to admit that I grieved God after I was converted, and that makes me less than they."

The others were no better

Her humble admission is touching. But if the truth were known about any of the saints of God, Theresa's confession would be their confession, too!

I wish it were possible to anoint the head of every Christian preacher so that he would never sin again while the world stands. Perhaps some would consider that a happy way to deal with the subject. But, in fact, if any person can be removed from the possibility of sin, he or she can only be some kind of a robot run by pulleys, wheels and push-buttons. A person morally incapable of doing evil would be, by the same token, morally incapable of doing good. A free human will is necessary to the concept of morality. I repeat: If our wills are not free to do evil, neither are they free to do good.

That is why I cannot accept the premise that our Lord Jesus Christ could not sin. If He could not sin, then the temptation in the desert was a farce, and God was a party to it. No. As a human being He *could* have sinned, but the fact that He *would not* sin marked Him as the holy Man He was.

It is not the inability to sin that makes a person holy, but his or her unwillingness to sin. A holy person is not one who cannot sin, but one who will not sin.

A truthful person is not one who cannot talk. He or she is one who can talk and could lie, but will not. An honest person is not one who is in jail where he or she cannot be dishonest. An honest person is one who is free to be dishonest, but will not be.

The Old Testament priest, set apart to serve his fellow Israelites and represent them before the Lord, had the potential of himself becoming unholy through sin. Had he been nothing more than a robot, incapable of sin, he would never have understood the needs and the guilt of the people he served. He never could have entered into their difficulties and troubles. A physician who himself has never felt any pain surely could never sympathize with an ailing, suffering patient.

But what was the sinning priest to do? Should he give up to discouragement? Should he resign himself to failure? No! There was a remedy. And what about ministers and all of God's servants today? In a time of temptation and failure, should they simply quit? Should they write a letter of resignation and walk out, saying, "I am not an Augustine or a Wesley; therefore, I give up"? No, if they are aware of what the Word of God says, they will seek God's remedy.

The Old Testament remedy

The remedy for the Old Testament spiritual leader was clear:

> He must bring to the Lord a young bull without defect as a sin offering for the sin he has committed. He is to present the bull at the entrance to the Tent of Meeting before the Lord. He is to lay his hand on its head and slaughter it before the Lord. Then the anointed priest shall take some of the bull's blood and carry it into the Tent of Meeting. He is to dip his finger into the blood and sprinkle some of it seven times before the Lord, in front of the curtain of the sanctuary. The priest shall then put some of the blood on the horns of the altar of fragrant incense that is before the Lord in the Tent of Meeting. The rest of the bull's blood he shall pour out at the base of the altar of burnt offering at the entrance of the Tent of Meeting. (4:3–7)

That was how an Old Testament priest atoned for his sin. The Lord God was providing a day-by-day remedy for spiritual weakness and failure.

What if the entire congregation of Israel sinned? Was there recourse for them? Yes.

If the whole Israelite community sins unintentionally and does what is forbidden in any of the Lord's commands, even though the community is unaware of the matter, they are guilty. When they become aware of the sin they committed, the assembly must bring a young bull as a sin offering and present it before the Tent of Meeting. The elders of the community are to lay their hands on the bull's head before the Lord, and the bull shall be slaughtered before the Lord. (4:13–14)

And, again, the same procedure follows as for the priest who has sinned. God says, "In this way the priest will make atonement for them, and they will be forgiven" (4:20).

Leaders were not exempt

There was still another category of people said to be in need of a sin remedy: the rulers or leaders. Here is the procedure God outlined for them:

When a leader sins unintentionally and does what is forbidden in any of the commands of the Lord his God, he is guilty. When he is made aware of the sin he committed, he must bring as his offering a male goat without defect. He is to lay his hand on the goat's head and slaughter it at the place where the burnt offering is slaughtered before the Lord. It is a sin offering. (4:23–24)

And, again, the same procedure for making atonement follows.

So God, in His Old Testament Law, made provision for the offending person or persons to be forgiven and restored, whether priest, ruler, the whole community or an individual member of the community. Note in regard to the individual who sinned, he was to take steps to atone for his failure "when he is made aware of the sin he committed" (4:28). This speaks of the person's conscience awaking to the fact that he or she sinned. In the Gospels, we read of the willful prodigal who left his father and went into a far country. But at last he came to himself and acknowledged his guilt. Prior to that awakening, he had been just as thoroughly a sinner, but he would not acknowledge it or confess it.

I delight in these instructions of the Lord to the common people because I love the common people. In using the term, I do not mean "common" in the sense of ugliness, ignorance, crudeness or vulgarity. But when I think of the common people so much loved by our Lord Jesus, I think of people like you and me. We make up that great throng of folks who are entirely without fame. We probably never will have our names in *Who's Who*, or win a Nobel or Pulitzer prize. We are the plain people—just the great multitude of common folks that God made!

When we look at a prize chrysanthemum in a flower show or florist's window, we are astonished at the beauty of the bloom. Much professional help goes into the propagation of a chrysanthemum. But for simple, plain people, I recommend a wide expanse of daisies nodding in the balmy, summer sun. They are among the common flowers—plain, simple blooms—and they do not have an inflated price tag!

Moreover, daisies do not require anything but God's spacious heaven above and His bright sunshine. They will sway there in the gentle breeze in all their natural beauty. They have been around for centuries, and they will still be here in centuries to come, if the Lord tarries. They do not require much. They are the common flowers.

The delight of a spring wild flower

I like flowers, whatever their origin, but I get more delight from discovering a common wild flower in the spring when I am scarcely expecting it than in a bouquet from the florist that has been carefully tended by horticulturists. And the wild flower costs me nothing—just the effort to see it, that is all.

In the spiritual realm, I guess God has His chrysanthemums. We read the stories of the great saints, and I am an admirer of every one of them. Perhaps in the long run, however, I am more at home with God's common daisy varieties than I am with the carefully cultivated churchmen who have been His showpieces for centuries. Think how tragic it would be if we had to say to God, "Now, God, we just have a few Christians that we can call to your attention. We mention Paul and Chrysostom and Augustine and Francis. We will add Luther and Wesley and Knox. That is about all we can muster."

I am sure God would smile and reply, "No, those are just My prize chrysanthemums. They were some of the great ones. I am glad for them, but I am not so poverty stricken for spiritual leadership that I must depend just on those." And then He reveals to us an innumerable company that no one can number—common flowers of field and meadow that just somehow took root and grew in the sunshine and looked heavenward and gathered the rain and the dew and loved God for His own sake.

These are men and women whose hands may be grimy from toil. Perhaps they do not understand all the learned allusions of the highly-educated preacher. They may not have any diplomas or degrees. But they bear the likeness of the family of God. They may have grown up where they had little opportunity to cultivate themselves as the more famous did. But they are true to God. They are the plain, common people—the simple, unknown millions willing to share their fragrance even in the desert places. They are my kind of people—every time!

When I am with some of the well-known preachers, I sit down and talk with them, if they are willing. If we can talk about God or faith or good books, we hit it off for a while. But mostly I wander off to hunt up some butcher from Atlanta or a carpenter from Detroit or perhaps a factory worker from Akron or a machinist from Minneapolis or a hog farmer from Ottumwa. I feel more at home among them because they are God's plain, common people. I am thankful that there are so many of them!

You may be the transgressor

But not infrequently, one of these "members of the community" sins. Perhaps *you* are the one. Should this be the signal to surrender to discouragement? Should this be the time to give up, declaring the Christian life impossible, the temptations too great, the world too tough? No! God says there is a remedy if you sin through ignorance and find yourself guilty of tresspassing one of the commandments. You are to bring a sin offering.

For the Israelites, it was a financially costly procedure. In the case of a sinning priest, it meant the price of a young bull. For a rank-and-file individual, it meant the price of a female goat. Today, the offering is in no sense monetary. And no man of God will ever trick you into believing that your monetary gift will serve as atonement for sin.

But, bring your offering! In this era of God's grace, an offering has already been made. "Look, the Lamb of God, who takes away the sin of the world!" (John 1:29). You do not have to search for a bull or a goat. Your sacrifice has been made once and is efficacious forever!

> Not all the blood of beasts on Jewish altars slain
> Could give the guilty conscience peace, or wash away the stain.
> But Christ, the heavenly Lamb, takes all our sins away;
> A sacrifice of nobler name and richer blood than they!

Continuing, Isaac Watts, that man of God, confessed,

> My faith would lay her hand on that dear head of Thine;
> While like a penitent I stand, and there confess my sin.

My soul looks back to see the burden Thou
didst bear,
When hanging on the accursed tree, and
knows her guilt was there!

So, in the covenant of grace, you need only to lay
your hand on the head of the divine Sin Offering,
the Lamb that was provided. What does that mean
to us? It means identification.

Identification and union

In the New Testament there is much said about
the laying on of hands. It was symbolic of identification and union. We lay our hands on the head of
a young minister being ordained as we identify
ourselves with him and with others who laid their
hands on our heads—a holy succession through
the years. The Israelite who recognized his or her
guilt was to lay his or her hands on the head of the
offering, thus identifying with the sacrifice. That
common man or woman was saying, "God, I deserve to die, for I sinned. Through faith in the mystery of atonement, I am going to live, and this female goat will die. I lay my hand on its head and
confess my sin, in effect putting my sin on the animal sacrifice."

In the repetition of that ritual, God was telling
Israel that one day a perfect Lamb would come who
would not symbolically but actually take away sin—
"a sacrifice of nobler name and richer blood!" He—
Jesus—"is the atoning sacrifice for our sins, and not
only for ours but also for the sins of the whole
world."

Sometimes when I am alone with my Bible, I get

on my knees and turn to Isaiah 53. For every first-person pronoun in that chapter I substitute all three of my names. "Surely he took up Aiden Wilson Tozer's infirmities / and carried Aiden Wilson Tozer's sorrows. . . . / He was pierced for Aiden Wilson Tozer's transgressions, / he was crushed for Aiden Wilson Tozer's iniquities. . . ." That is laying your hand on the head of the Sacrifice. That is identifying with the dying Lamb.

You can do it today — now!

The Resurrection of Christ: More Than a Festival

The angel said to the women, "Do not be afraid, for I know that you are looking for Jesus, who was crucified. He is not here; he has risen, just as he said. Come and see the place where he lay. Then go quickly and tell his disciples: 'He has risen from the dead and is going ahead of you into Galilee. There you will see him.' " (Matthew 28:5–7)

ANY CHRISTIAN CHURCH DOLEFULLY preoccupied with the crucifixion of Jesus Christ rather than pressing forward in the blessed life of the risen Savior is dispensing what one person described as a "pitying kind of religion." I cannot tolerate a pitying kind of religion.

True spiritual power does not reside in the ancient cross but in the victory of the mighty, resurrected Lord of Glory who could pronounce after spoiling death: "All authority in heaven and on earth has been given to me" (Matthew 28:18). Of this we need to be thoroughly convinced. Our power as Christians does not lie in the manger at Bethlehem or in the relics of Golgotha's cross. Our power lies in the eternal Christ who triumphed over death.

When Jesus died on the cross, He died in weakness. When Jesus arose from the grave, He arose in power. If we forget or deny the truth and glory of Jesus' resurrection and His present place at God's right hand, we lose all the significance of Christianity!

The resurrection of Jesus Christ brought about some startling changes of direction. It is both interesting and profitable to look through the eyes of Matthew at those women who played a significant role in the resurrection drama.

First, the women came *to* the tomb. They came in love, but they came also in sadness and fear. They were there to mourn. That was the direction of their religion before they knew Jesus had been raised from the dead. Their orientation was toward the tomb that they supposed held the body of Jesus.

People's orientation is still toward the tomb

People all around us still face the direction of the tomb, knowing only mourning and grief, uncertainty and the fear of death. But on that historic resurrection day, the faithful women had a dramatic change of direction. They heard the angelic news and they saw the evidence: "He is not here," the angels informed the women; "he has risen, just as he said" (Matthew 28:8). The mammoth stone covering the tomb had been rolled away. They themselves could see the stark emptiness of the sepulchre.

"Go quickly and tell his disciples," the angels continued. Matthew tells us the women "hurried away" *from* the tomb. What an amazing change of direction brought about by the angels' good news! Instead of going *to* the tomb, they now hurry *from* the tomb. The tomb was empty—stripped of its age-old power. The women had been sure they were seeing the end of Jesus' life three days before as He hung on the cross and gasped, "It is finished." Now they began to realize the endlessness—the eternity of life and victory—that His resurrection had made possible.

If this is not the message and meaning of Easter, the Christian church is involved in a shallow one-day festival each year, intent upon the brightness of colors, the fragrance of flowers, the sweet sentiments of poetry and the heady stirrings of spring. But Easter is not just a day in the church calendar—a celebration in and of itself. That first resurrection morning was the beginning of something grand and vast that has never ended and will not end. And the commission the risen and ascending Christ gave to His followers is still the church's great worldwide missionary responsibility, as valid today as then. The church needs to reorder its priorities.

The resurrection of Christ is not some part of our world's complex and continuing mythology. It is not a Santa Claus tale. It is history. It is reality.

Strip the church of the historicity of Jesus Christ's bodily resurrection, and it is helpless and hopeless. The true church is necessarily founded on the verity of the resurrection. Jesus died a real death. There was a real tomb and a real stone to seal the tomb. But, thank God, there was also a real resurrection! The sovereign Father in heaven sent an angel to roll the stone away. Out from that now empty

grave burst forth a resurrected Savior able to proclaim to His disciples, "All authority in heaven and
on earth has been given to me."

Radiant, beckoning opportunities

Little wonder that true Christians do not spend
their time enlisting sympathy for a dying Jesus:
"Let us kneel by the cross and weep awhile." The
church has too many radiant, beckoning opportu-
nities to be occupied with things like that. We shall
not join with those who regard Jesus as a martyr, a
victim of His own zeal, a poor pitable Man with
good intentions who found the world too big and
life too much for Him.

Too many artists still picture Jesus sinking down
in a helplessness wrought by death. Why should
we in His church walk around in black, continuing
to grieve at the tomb? The record clearly announces
that He came back from death to prove His words,
"All authority in heaven and on earth has been
given to me."

Jesus died for us—true—but ever since the hour
of resurrection, He has been the mighty Jesus, the
mighty Christ, the mighty Lord! Authority does
not lie with a Babe in a manger. Authority does not
lie with a Man nailed helplessly to a cross. Authority lies with the resurrected Man who was once in
that manger, who hung on that cross but who, after
He gave His life, arose on the third day, later ascending to the right hand of the Father. In Him lies
all authority.

Our business is not to mourn beside the grave.
Our business is to thank God with tearful reverence that Jesus was willing to go into that grave.

Our business is to thank God for an understanding of what the cross means and what the resurrection means both to God and to us.

Do we rightly understand the resurrection? It placed a glorious crown upon all of Christ's sufferings. Do we realize the full significance of Jesus Christ's being seated today at the Father's right hand—seated in absolute majesty and kingly power, sovereign over every power in heaven and on earth?

Always there are those with a rejoinder: "But how can you back up that big talk? If Christ is sovereign over all the world, what about—" And they mention the latest enclave of tension and bloodletting. "What about Communism?" "What about hydrogen bombs and impending doom?" "If Christ is sovereign, why is there a continuing armaments race?" "Why does the Middle East situation continue to plague our world?"

God's plan is on schedule

There is an answer. It is the answer of the prophetic Scriptures. God has a plan in His dealing with the nations of the world and their governments. God's plan is on schedule, and it will continue to be so. His plan has always called for the return of Israel to Palestine. The nations of the earth are playing themselves into position all over the world—almost like a giant checkerboard—while God waits sovereignly for the consummation.

While Israel continues to gather, while the king of the north beats himself out, the Christian church prays and labors to evangelize the world for the Savior.

And Christ waits. The One with all authority waits to exercise that authority universally. But in the life and ministry of His church He is showing His authority in many ways. I suspect He would show it in many more ways if His church only believed that He could and would!

When Jesus announced, "All authority in heaven and on earth has been given to me," what did He expect His followers to do? What are the implications for all of us who are in the body of Christ?

The answer is rather plain. Jesus followed that announcement by a command: "Therefore go and make disciples of all nations, baptizing them in the name of the Father and of the Son and of the Holy Spirit, and teaching them to obey everything I have commanded you" (Matthew 28:19–20).

Therefore is the word that connects things together. Christ has been given all authority; therefore we are to go and make disciples of all nations. All of the implications of the resurrection add up to the fact that the Christian church must be a missionary church if it is to meet the expectations of its risen Savior.

Because He is alive forevermore, Jesus could promise, in the same context as His command, that He would be with us always, even unto the end of the age. There are countless Lo-I-am-with-you-alway wall plaques and mottos in Christian homes. But the text, from the familiar King James version of the Bible, is only a partial quotation, and it overrides certain implications. We believers are skilled in using the knife of bad teaching to separate a little passage from its context, much as we might separate a slice of orange from its rind. We segregate the promise and put it on our mottoes and calendars. But in this case, let us honestly be open to what our Lord wants to say to us.

Not exactly

Is this *exactly* what our Lord said: "Lo, I am with you alway"? Not exactly. He actually said, "Go and make disciples of all nations, baptizing them in the name of the Father and of the Son and of the Holy Spirit, and teaching them to obey everything I have commanded you. And surely I am with you always, to the very end of the age." That little word *and* is not there by accident. Jesus was saying that His presence was assured in the Christian church if the church continued faithfully in its missionary responsibilities.

That is why I say that the resurrection of Jesus Christ is something more than making us the happiest people in the Easter parade. Are we to listen to a cantata, join in singing "Up from the Grave He Arose," smell the lilies and go home and forget it? No, certainly not!

The resurrection of Jesus Christ lays hold on us with all the authority of sovereign obligation. It says that the Christian church is to go and make disciples—to go and make disciples of all nations. The moral obligation of the resurrection of Christ is the missionary obligation—the responsibility and privilege of personally carrying the message, of interceding for those who go, of being involved financially in the cause of world evangelization.

Many times I have asked myself how professing Christians can relegate the great missionary imperative of our Lord to the sidelines of their church's activity. I cannot follow the reasoning of those who teach that the missionary commission given by Jesus Christ does not belong to the church but will be carried out during the days of "great tribulation" emphasized in Bible prophecy.

I refuse to give in to the devil's deceitful tactics that keep the church of Jesus Christ satisfied with an Easter celebration devoid of the power of the resurrection. The enemy of our souls is quite happy to let Christians make a big thing of Easter Sunday, putting the emphasis on flowers and cantatas and insipid sermons that refer to Jesus Christ as the greatest of earth's heroes. The devil is willing to settle for all of that display as long as churches stop short of telling the whole truth about Jesus Christ and His resurrection from the dead. But he is mortally afraid when churches begin to really believe that Jesus is now seated in the place of authority at God's right hand and that he—Satan—is actually a frightened fugitive.

Satan intends to distract us

It is Satan's business to keep Christians mourning awhile and weeping with pity beside the cross instead of demonstrating that Jesus Christ is risen indeed, has ascended to heaven and at the precise prophetic time will return to earth to chain Satan and hurl him into hell. Satan will do almost anything to keep us from actually believing that death has no more dominion, that Jesus Christ has been given all authority in heaven and on earth, that He holds in His hands the keys to hell.

When will the Christian church awake and get on the offensive for its risen and ascended Savior? It will be when the church comes to know the full meaning of the cross and to experience the implication and power of the resurrection among its members—that is when. Through the power of Christ's resurrection we must take the spiritual offensive, we must become the aggressors and our witness must become the positive force it should be in reaching the ends of the earth with the gospel.

Jesus Christ asks us to surrender to His Lordship and to obey His commands. He will supply the power if we will believe His promises and demonstrate the reality of His resurrection.

Actually, His promises have taken the strain and pressure from our missionary responsibility. When the Spirit of God speaks, dealing with men and women about their personal missionary responsibility, Christ assures them of His presence and power as they prepare to go.

"All authority in heaven and on earth has been given to me. No longer am I in the grave. With all authority I can protect you. I can support you. I can go ahead of you. I can make your witness and ministry effective. *Therefore go and make disciples of all nations, baptizing them, . . . teaching them.* I will go with you. I will never leave you nor forsake you. *I am with you always, to the very end of the age."*

In time of war and in other circumstances, men without God suffer alone and die alone, all alone. But it can never be said that any true soldier of the cross of Jesus Christ goes forth into missionary service alone. In the annals of missionary history there have been many Christian martyrs, but not one of them died alone. Jesus Christ keeps His promise. Jesus Christ leads those martyrs in triumph through death to the world beyond.

Do you see it? Resurrection is more than a day of celebration. It is an obligation that we must understand and accept. Because Jesus Christ is alive, there is something for us to do for Him. We dare not settle back in religious apathy.

Believe Jesus! Trust the Risen One who said, "All authority in heaven and on earth has been given to me. Therefore go and make disciples of all nations. . . . And surely I am with you always, to the very end of the age."

9

Christian Uniformity: An Evangelical Answer

Finally, all of you, live in harmony with one another; be sympathetic, love as brothers. (1 Peter 3:8)

EVANGELICAL CHRISTIANS TEND TO PAY little attention to religious trends and fads outside their own boundaries. One of these in our day is an emphasis on church unity. In the face of this insistence in some quarters that everyone in the church ought to be just like everyone else, it is only fair that evangelicals have an opportunity to respond. This is one response.

That the Bible teaches Christian unity we are agreed. But the unity taught in the Scriptures can only come through genuine love and sincere compassion within the Christian fellowship. It can only come through the work of God in the heart of each believer—and then there can be unity even where there is a blessed and free diversity!

There is in Christian literature a statement by an old bishop that the uniformity we desire in the Christian church is not just a matter of achieving "solidarity." He reminds us that anyone can achieve a solid unity out of variety just by the freezing process! We can distinguish this kind of frozen unity in the conduct of those churches where no one ever disagrees with anyone else because they all agreed to hold no basic tenets or positive beliefs. "Doctrine really does not matter that much anyhow," is their explanation.

But the apostle Peter writes to believers about the reality of living "in harmony with one another." Leading commentators tell us the expression literally means to be unanimous. So let me tell you what being unanimous is not, in order that we may discover what Christian unanimity or harmony really is.

Being unanimous—spiritual unanimity—does not involve a regulated uniformity. I cannot comprehend how the churches have fallen into the error of believing that unanimity means uniformity. Some actually hold that to be like-minded involves imposing a similarity from the outside. This has been a great error—the belief that harmony within religious bodies can be secured by imposing uniformity.

Uniformity cannot be imposed

Look at the word *uniform*. In one use, it is an adjective describing a situation. But it is also a noun referring to identifying garments worn by members of certain groups. Our Armed Forces wear uniforms. Municipal police wear uniforms. Some delivery personnel are uniformed. Such garments provide uniformity—a uniformity imposed from the outside. But anyone who has ever served in the Armed Forces knows there is a world of disagreement and grousing among those who wear the uniforms. Merely putting on a uniform does not in any sense bring about a basic unity and harmony in any group of men and women.

Imposed uniformity is a great error because it assumes that uniformity is an external thing and that it can be achieved by imposition. It fails to acknowledge that the only valid unity is heart unity.

Actually, variety, not uniformity, is the hallmark of God. Wherever you see God's hand, you see variety rather than uniformity. Paul comments that stars differ from one another in splendor. When the smoke, grime and smog lying over our urban centers lift a bit, and we gaze at the stars spread out across the sky, we are looking at heavenly bodies no two of which are exactly alike.

If God had made all the stars according to a uniform pattern and placed them equidistant from our earth, to look at the stars would be like gazing at a glaring theater marquee. I prefer the mysterious, wonderful sky we see on a clear night.

The same with leaves. If you are inclined to check, you can find out in five minutes that no two leaves on any tree are exactly alike. They all differ. They are somewhat alike—they may even be alike basically, but God allows them a certain freedom of variety.

Visit the ocean shore—any ocean shore—and you will see that even when the winds are high and the waves are running, no two waves are exactly alike. You may look carelessly as they roll in over the sand and think they are alike. But if you look more closely, you will agree that no two of them are alike. The artist who paints the ocean waves all alike has imposed something of his own mind upon the

Creator God's work, for the ocean never repeats the same size and shape of a wave, though the waves reach into numbers we are unable to count.

Even bird songs vary

Consider bird songs. We may hear a bird singing and be able to identify it. "That is a cardinal," we say—or a warbler, or a mourning dove, as the case may be. But those who have been trained to listen closely tell us that even among species, no two birds sing exactly alike.

When we reflect upon the Bible saints, we sometimes speak of the similarities between these personalities. But the differences are far more marked and apparent than the similarities. Who can conceive of two men more opposite than Isaiah and Elijah? If they had been sitting together in the same congregation, they would hardly have been recognized as belonging to the same race, let alone the same faith! Their similarities were within. They belonged together inside, but they certainly were different on the outside.

Or, contrast Peter and Moses. Or, stay within the little circle of Jesus' disciples, and compare Peter with Philip or John. Externally and in their character traits they were unlike each other. Internally there was unity produced by the same Master.

When God established His church, He established a church that was to be unanimous within. But it was a church with all the outward variety of an attractive flower garden.

I knew a dear man of God—a preacher of a different skin color from mine—who used to say to white audiences, "God makes His bouquets from the flowers which contain all His created colors. If they were all white, there would be no variety, so God put me here in your midst to provide variety!"

He was right. God has His own variety throughout all the church, everywhere—not only in looks but in personality, in taste, in gifts and in ministries.

And yet Peter encourages us to live in harmony— to be unanimous. What does he mean? He means that the Spirit of God making Christ real within our beings will make us alike in certain qualities and in disposition.

True Christian compassion is one of those qualities. Peter leaves us little doubt about the fruits of genuine Christian unanimity within. "Be sympathetic," he says, "love as brothers, be compassionate and humble. . . . repay evil . . . with blessing. . . . do good; . . . Seek peace" (1 Peter 3:8–11). That is the path to a blessed Christian unity and unanimity. That is the way to have one mind.

The kind of unity that matters

That was the kind of uniformity Peter was looking for among the followers of Christ. Every earnest believer must know the unanimity of compassion, the ability to love others, the uniformity of a spirit that reaches out in sympathy, the tenderness of heart that can express God's grace by forgiving others.

Are you willing to measure the compassion in your own spirit? Compassion means sympathetic understanding. Wherever one life touches another, there must be compassion if we are to please our Lord. This is what our true Christian unity demands—a likeness, a sympathetic understanding at every point where our hearts touch. In other matters there can be diversity and variety. But wherever we touch each other there is to be unity. The variety among God's believing children is in itself God's artistic plan to bring beauty to the church.

I suppose there never was a body of Christians that succeeded in being freer than the Quakers, even though they themselves did their best to choke that freedom. They imposed a uniform dress code. They imposed a non-ordinary way of speaking. But in spite of these practices, they had so much of the inner Flame that they succeeded in presenting to the world a wonderful flower-garden variety. So we are to have the compassion of Christ within us. At the point we touch a fellow believer, there is to be sympathetic understanding. In those areas where we do not touch, there may be diversity.

Peter also reminds us that we are to love one another "as brothers." This love speaks of oneness wherever hearts touch. It is a true and blessed unity made possible through the bonds of God's love. This is God's way—the genuine way—of bringing people together in a unity that is living and that will abide.

Now, without any desire to be disruptive, I must ask a question about the many insistent demands for getting everyone into a single, worldwide Christian church: "Why is it that the generation talking the most about unity is also the generation with the greatest amount of hate and suspicion and the generation with the biggest bombs and the largest armies?"

There is no unity in the world

They cannot fool me! I refuse to be taken in by all of the smooth talk and gentle assurances that "all men are brothers and we must forget our differences because of the Fatherhood of God and the brotherhood of man." They do not fool me because I know there is no unity in the world. There is division, hatred, hostility and open strife. When these people say, "Let's forget all the differences," I just want the opportunity to see if that lump under their coat is still there—the lump that is a revolver!

God's love shed abroad in our hearts—a love that can only be conveyed to us by the Spirit of Jesus Christ, our Lord—is the only means of true unity among men and women today. All other emphasis on unity is a sadly strange and ironic joke that must have had its origin in hell below.

Is it possible to be a believing child of God and not be tenderhearted? When Peter advises that Christians are to be "sympathetic" one toward the other, he is actually saying that our hearts are to be tender toward each other. Religion will either make us very tender of heart, considerate and kind, or it will make us very hard.

Anyone who has studied history knows that men and women—religious men and women—can be very severe, engaging in the worst of cruelties, explaining it all in the name of religion and the "principle" involved. I have a question that I ask myself in this regard: "Whose side am I on—principle or people?" Within the history of our own American government, we bow in respect to one of our great presidents who was a man first and president second. They called him Honest Abe. He had a gift for sensing the humorous in life and a heart that cried easily over other people's sorrows.

During the Civil War, Abraham Lincoln had to deal with the military leaders who stood on ceremony and acted on principle in their treatment of young lads taken out of the hills and away from the farms, conscripted and sent with little training to the front lines of battle. When the terror of gunfire and the screaming of the dying became overpowering, some of the boys turned away and fled in fear. When they were caught, they were sentenced to die.

Lincoln tried to save them

Along with his many other duties, Lincoln was busy doing what he could to save these young men. One day his associates found him sadly turning over papers from a file and writing something at the bottom of each, one after the other.

"What are you doing, Mr. President?" one of his associates asked.

"Tomorrow is 'butcher day' in the Army," Lincoln replied. "They are going to shoot my boys, so I have been going over their papers once more to see if I can't get some of them off."

We love and honor the memory of Abraham Lincoln for that kind of spirit. He was a man who loved people and was not ashamed to be tender in heart and full of pity for those in need. I do not mention Lincoln here to imply that he was a great Christian, for I am not a judge of that. But he was a great man and he had much that we Christians could borrow. I am convinced that he was a tender hearted, pitying man who put people ahead of principle!

I do not have to tell you that principle has been a hard, rough cross upon which human beings have been nailed throughout the centuries. "There's a principle involved," zealous men have always cried as they executed the unfortunate victim. The person's blood and tears and sweat never affected them at all because their pride assured them that they were acting on principle.

Let people argue as they will; it is not principle that holds the moral world together, but rather the presence of a holy God and love for God and mankind! To be sure, moral laws exist in the world, and no one preaches that with any greater emphasis than I do. But to extract the principle from the holy and loving heart of God and then nail men on it is a far cry from the teaching and example of our Lord Jesus Christ.

Jesus Himself never spent His time talking about principles. He always talked about people. Even in His illustrative stories, the parables—He was not citing principles. He was talking about people. Someone was in trouble, someone had gone astray or was lost, someone had been sent out to bring other people in. Always there were people.

Make of this what you will, but I do not think I would offer to give my life for a principle. I trust I would die for those I love. I trust I would die for the church of Jesus Christ. I trust I would give my everything for the love of God and the love of mankind. If I did not, I would surely be ashamed.

Jesus did not arrive riding a "principle"

Now, that is one thing, but it is quite another to extract a stiff, ironclad principle and then nail a man on it. God's Word tells us to be sympathetic, compassionate, humble. Jesus did not come down from His place in glory riding on a steel beam of divine principle—hard and stiff and cold. He was full of pity and love, tender hearted and submissive to the will of His Father on behalf of mankind. He went from the womb of the Virgin to the cross on Golgotha.

Of course, Jesus died for the moral government of Almighty God, but it was people He cared for and served. He achieved His end not by hardness and harshness and legal principles, but by love and care and compassion for people. Back of it all, certainly, was the unchanging, divine principle—the moral righteousness of God—for the holiness of Deity must be sustained even if the world falls.

But being our divine Savior and Lord, Jesus walked in and out of His experiences with men and women with all sweetness and tenderness, never leaving an irritation or a scratch. We could well say that love lubricated His spirit. He loved people—men, women and children, the low as well as the high.

There is nothing that will make us more tender of heart and more compassionate in spirit than true religion—the true reception of the mercies of God. The Word of God plainly teaches that God our Father wants us to have true spiritual unity—to experience the divine sensitivity that makes it possible for us to live in harmony with one another.

But in the New Testament record, we also see in contrast the proud and unbending religion of the Pharisees—and how it brought hardness of heart to them.

Religion will do the one thing or the other. I want to be on the side of the sympathetic and compassionate. How about you?

CHAPTER

10

The Presence of Christ: Meaning of the Communion

For I received from the Lord what I also passed on to you: The Lord Jesus, on the night he was betrayed, took bread, and when he had given thanks, he broke it and said, "This is my body, which is for you; do this in remembrance of me." In the same way, after supper he took the cup, saying, "This cup is the new covenant in my blood; do this, whenever you drink it, in remembrance of me." For whenever you eat this bread and drink this cup, you proclaim the Lord's death until he comes. . . . anyone who eats and drinks without recognizing the body of the Lord eats and drinks judgment on himself. (1 Corinthians 11:23–29)

IT IS AMAZING THAT MANY PEOPLE regard the Christian church as just another institution and the observance of Communion as just one of its periodic rituals. Any genuine, New Testament church actually *is* communion. It is not an institution. The Bible makes that plain.

One of the dictionary definitions of *communion* is a body of Christians having a common faith. Sharing and participation are other terms used in defining *communion*. Regardless of traditions and terminology, the basic question whenever we approach the Lord's table is this: "Have we come together to celebrate the Presence of our divine Lord and risen Savior?"

Blessed is the congregation that has found the spiritual maturity and understanding to honestly confess, "Our congregation is so keenly aware of the presence of Jesus in our midst that our entire fellowship is an unceasing communion!" What a joyful experience it is for us in this church age to be part of a congregation drawn together by the desire to know God's presence, to sense His nearness.

The observance of Communion will have no ultimate meaning for us if we do not believe that our Lord Jesus Christ is literally present in the body of Christ on earth—His true church. But note my important distinction: Christ is *literally* present with us, not physically present.

Some people approach the communion table with an awe that is almost fear. They think they are approaching the physical presence of God. But it is a mistake to imagine that He is physically present.

In the Old Testament instance of the burning bush, God was not physically present. Neither was He physically present under the wings of the cherubim in the tabernacle's Most Holy Place, nor in the cloud by day and fire by night that guided Israel through the desert. But He was present—literally present. So today, God who became Man—the Man who is God—this Man who is the focal point of divine manifestation is here! When we come to the Lord's table, we do not have to try to bring His presence. He is there!

We are to discern Christ's presence

God does ask, however, that we bring to the Communion the kind of faith that will discern Christ's presence. He asks us to bring the kind of faith that will enable us to obey the New Testament prompting, "Forgiving each other, just as in Christ God forgave you" (Ephesians 4:32). Out of our worship and from the Communion, God wants us to be able to sense the loving nearness of the Savior—instantaneously bestowed!

There is nothing else like this in the world. Imagine the God who made the universe, who holds the world in His hands, standing ready to baptize us with a sense of His presence. Sensing that Presence will completely change our lives. It will elevate us, purify us and deliver us from the domination of carnal flesh to the point where our lives will be a continuing, radiant fascination to others.

Even a cursory reading of Paul's first letter to the Corinthians alerts us to trouble in that early church congregation. For one thing, the members came together for reasons other than to recognize the divine Presence. Paul said they met "without recognizing the body of the Lord." I have checked many sources of Christian scholarship, and I agree with Ellicott and other commentators who believe this means the Corinthians met "without recognizing the Presence." They were not required to believe that the bread and the wine were God, but they were required to believe that God was present when Christians met to eat the bread and drink the wine.

Because they refused to recognize God's presence, the Corinthian Christians were in great spiritual trouble. Actually, they were coming together for purposes other than to meet God. There was a judgment upon them because they were too carnal, too worldly, too socially minded, too unspiritual to recognize that when Christians meet they should at least have the reverence that a Greek had when he led a heifer to the sacred grove. They should at least have the reverence that a Greek poet had when he quietly composed poems to his deity. They should at least have the reverence of an Old Testament high priest when he entered the Most Holy Place and put blood beneath the cherubim-shaded cover of the Ark.

But the Corinthians came with another attitude. They did not come to commune with the Presence, and so the meaning and purpose of the Communion became vague.

Today, I say, we ought to be a company of believers drawn together to meet the God who appeared in flesh. That God-Man is not a preacher or an elder or a deacon, but Jesus Christ, risen from the dead and eternally alive! It is impossible to separate the Communion from the centrality of Jesus Christ, the revealed Word of God.

Some think of Communion as a celebration — and in the very best sense it is. We gather to celebrate our Lord Jesus Christ. In order for us to grasp the spirit of this celebration, notice the relationship of Christ, the Son of Man, to five words with prepositions attached.

Devotion To

First, we celebrate Christ's *devotion to* His Father's will. Our Lord Jesus Christ had no secondary aims. His one passion in life was the fulfillment of His Father's will. Of no other human being can this be said in absolute terms. Others have been devoted to God, but never absolutely. Always there has been occasion to mourn the introduction, however brief, of some distraction. But Jesus was never distracted. Never once did He deviate from His Father's will. It was always before Him, and it was to this one thing that He was devoted.

Because it was not the Father's will that any should perish, Jesus was devoted to the rescue of fallen mankind—completely devoted to it. He did not do a dozen other things as avocations. He did that one thing that would permit a Holy God to forgive sin. He was devoted to the altar of sacrifice so that mankind might be rescued from the wages of sin.

One of the old Baptist missionary societies had as its symbol an ox quietly standing between a plow and an altar. Underneath was the legend: "Ready for either or for both!" Plow, if that be God's will. Die on the altar, if that be God's will. Plow awhile, and then die on the altar. I can think of no more perfect symbol of devotion to God.

That symbol certainly describes the attitude of our Lord Jesus Christ. He was ready first for His labors on earth, the work with the plow. And He was ready for the altar of sacrifice—the cross. With no side interests, He moved with steady purpose—almost with precision—toward the cross. He would not be distracted or turned aside. He was completely devoted to the cross, completely devoted to the rescue of mankind, because He was completely devoted to His Father's will.

Even "if we are faithless," as the ancient hymn puts it (2 Timothy 2:13), Jesus' faithful devotion is unchanged. He has not changed. And He will not change. He is as devoted now as He was then. He came to earth to be a Devoted One, for the word *devoted* actually is a religious term referring usually to an animal, often a lamb, that was selected and marked for sacrifice to a god. So, our Lord Jesus Christ, the Lamb of God, was devoted—completely devoted—to be the Infinite Sacrifice for sin.

Separation from

The second phrase is *separation from*. There are many ways in which our Lord deliberately separated Himself from those around Him. We might say He separated Himself from people for people. Jesus did not separate Himself from people because He was weary of them, or because He disliked them. Rather, it was because He loved them. It was a separation in order that He might do for them what they could not do for themselves. He was the only one who could rescue them.

Throughout history there have been those who have separated themselves from people for other reasons. Tymen of Athens turned sour on the human race and went up into the hills. He separated himself from mankind because he hated the human race. But the separation of Jesus Christ from people was the result of love. He separated Himself from them for them. It was for them He came—and died. It was for them that He arose and ascended. For them He intercedes at the right hand of God.

Separation from is a phrase that marked Jesus. He not only kept Himself separated from sinners in the sense that He did not partake of their sins, but He was separated from the snare of trivialities. We Christians do so many things that are not really bad; they are just trivial. They are unworthy of us— much as if we discovered Albert Einstein cutting out paper dolls.

Our minds may not be among the six greatest of the ages, but like Einstein's, our minds have endless capabilities. Our spirits were designed by God to communicate with Deity. Yet we consume our time in trivialities. Jesus was never so engaged. He escaped the snare of trivialities. He was separated from the vanities of the human race. Need I remind you in this context that if these words characterized Jesus, they must also characterize each of us who claims to be a follower of Jesus? The runner separates himself from street clothes in order to free himself for the race. The soldier separates himself from civilian garb in order to don equipment that helps his mission of combat. So we as God's loving disciples must separate ourselves from everything that hinders our devotion to God.

Devotion to: the Father's will, the rescue of mankind from sin's entrapment, any necessary sacrifice. *Separation from:* sin, sinners who would be a snare to us, trivialities that would divert us from the important matters.

Three other phrases

I more quickly mention three other phrases in

addition to these two. The third is *rejection by.* Jesus suffered rejection by mankind because of His holiness. On the cross He suffered rejection by God the Father because He was ladened with our sins. He was vicariously sinful. "God made him who had no sin to be sin for us, so that in him we might become the righteousness of God" (2 Corinthians 5:21).

In that sense, Jesus suffered a twofold rejection. He was too holy to be received by sinful men. And in that awful moment of His sacrifice He was too sinful to be received by a holy God. So He hung between heaven and earth, rejected by both until He cried, "It is finished. . . . Father, into your hands I commit my spirit" (John 19:30; Luke 23:46). Then He was received by the Father.

But while He was bearing my sins—and yours— He was rejected by the Father. While He moved among men He was rejected by them because His holy life was a constant rebuke to them.

The fourth phrase is *identification with.* Surely Jesus was identified with us. Everything He did was for us; He acted in our stead. He took our guilt. He gave us His righteousness. In all that Jesus did on earth, He acted for us because by His incarnation He identified Himself with the human race. In His death and resurrection He identified Himself with the redeemed human race.

As a blessed result, whatever He is we are. Where He is, potentially His people are. What He is, potentially His people are—only His deity excepted.

Finally, consider His *acceptance at.* Jesus Christ, our Lord, has acceptance at the throne of God. Although once "rejected by," He is now "accepted at"! The bitter rejection has turned into joyous acceptance. And the same is true for His people. Through Him we died. Identified with Him, we live. And in our identification with Him we are accepted at the right hand of God the Father.

This is the meaning of our Communion celebration. Surely I do not need a picture of the holy family or a rosary to remind me of Jesus and His death on Calvary's cross. If my love for Jesus does not remind me 24 hours a day, then I need to confess and repent of my carelessness and ask for God's restoring grace and mercy that will keep me always in remembrance.

He went "astray"

One of the great Scottish dissenters who lived in the last century was Horatius Bonar. He belonged to the Free Church of Scotland, which came into being through a break with the state church. A critic of Bonar once said of him:

> Bonar was a wonderfully good man and a wonderfully gifted man, but his imagination led him astray. His imagination led him to believe that Jesus Christ was coming back to raise the dead and change the living. He was going to restore Israel to the Holy Land, transform the church and bless mankind, destroying the antichrist with the brightness of His coming.

Yes, it is too bad Bonar went so far "astray." In reply, I say that if Bonar went so far "astray" as to believe those things, perhaps that is why he could write hymns such as "I Heard the Voice of Jesus

Say, Come unto Me and Rest," and "I Lay My Sins on Jesus, the Spotless Lamb of God." Bonar also wrote a hymn about the Communion. Here it is:

> Here, O my Lord, I see Thee face to face;
>> Here would I touch and handle things unseen,
> Here grasp with firmer hand th'eternal grace,
>> And all my weariness upon Thee lean.
>
> Here would I feed upon the bread of God,
>> Here drink with Thee the royal wine of heaven;
> Here would I lay aside each earthly load,
>> Here taste afresh the calm of sins forgiven.
>
> This is the hour of banquet and of song;
>> This is the heavenly table spread for me;
> Here let me feast, and feasting, still prolong
>> The brief bright hour of fellowship with Thee.
>
> Too soon we rise; the symbols disappear;
>> The feast, though not the love, is past and gone;
> The bread and wine removed, but Thou art here,
>> Nearer than ever; still my Shield and Sun.
>
> Mine is the sin, but Thine the righteousness;
>> Mine is the guilt, but Thine the cleansing blood;
> Here is my robe, my refuge, and my peace,
>> Thy blood, Thy righteousness, O Lord my God.

Feast after feast thus comes and passes by,
  Yet passing, points to the glad feast above,
Giving sweet foretaste of the festal joy,
  The Lamb's great bridal feast of bliss and
  love.

The Lord's table, the Communion, is more than a picture on a wall, more than a set of beads reminding us of Jesus Christ and His death. It is a celebration of His person—a celebration in which we gladly join because we *do* remember Him. By it we testify to each other and to the world of Jesus' sacrificial, conquering death—until He comes!

Our Promised Hope:
We Shall Be Changed

As obedient children, do not conform to the evil desires you had when you lived in ignorance. But just as he who called you is holy, so be holy in all you do. (1 Peter 1:14–15)

THE CHRISTIAN CHURCH CANNOT EFFECTIVELY be Christ's church if it fails to firmly believe and boldly proclaim to every person: "You can be changed! You do not have to remain as you are!" That is a hope held out not just to the desperate drug addict and the helpless drunkard; it is valid for every person the world over.

Heed, therefore, what the Holy Spirit, in this apostolic injunction, is saying to us about human nature and God's grace. After all, the Scriptures allow no room for argument. We may have reason to disagree with a preacher's *interpretation* of the Scriptures, but once we know what the Holy Spirit has said, as believers we are committed to carry out the injunction without one word of objection. What else should we do with the Word of God but obey it?

"Do not conform to the evil desires you had when you lived in ignorance." Here is a truth nega-

tively stated but carrying with it a positive asser-
tion. If our conformity is not to be to our former evil
desires, to what or to whom is it to be? It is this
positive element that we consider. Certainly and
positively each of us is conforming to something or
someone. If not to the former evil desires, then
what?

Our English word, *conform*, expresses the apostle's admonition that Christian believers ought to
shape themselves according to a proper pattern.
"Conform to the right pattern" is what Peter actually was saying. In essence, he was also stressing a
most important fact: human nature is malleable —
it is not fixed and unchangeable, as many people
seem to believe. Perhaps clay is the very best illustration to help us to an understanding of this biblical principle.

Clay can be shaped

Clay is not fixed. It is malleable; it can be shaped.
After clay has been shaped by the potter, who gives
it the form he wants it to have, he puts it aside to
dry. Then he bakes it under intense heat, sometimes also adding a glaze, which is also baked on.

That piece of clay, once so malleable, is now per-
manently fixed. It is no longer subject to any
changes. Once clay has been baked and glazed, the
only way it can be changed is by destruction. The
object can be shattered and ruined, but it can never
be changed into something more beautiful or useful because it can never regain its malleable state.

For the apostle through the Holy Spirit to say,
"Do not conform," is indication that the baking-
glazing of our natures has not yet occurred. Thank-

fully, we are in a state of malleability regarding moral character.

There are two things that can be said to any person, whether an innocent youngster or a professional criminal on death row awaiting his fate for kidnapping and murder. The first is, "You can be changed!" The second, which is related, is this: "You are not finished yet!"

We hear much about people being hardened, but we should always remember that we need modifiers if we are going to get at the truth. When we say that a person is hardened and beyond help, we are saying that insofar as any power and influence we may have, the person probably is in a state beyond our changing. But actually and in truth, no one is beyond changing as long as he or she is alive and conscious!

In many cases, the hope may be dim, but the hope of change does exist for every person. It may be a dim hope for the alcoholic who allows herself only a few sober moments for serious thought, but she may be saved from complete despair by the knowledge that she can be changed. For the drug addict in frightful misery, who would sell his soul for the fix to carry him through one more day, that faint flicker of hope is all that may keep him from suicide.

Let us thank God for that kind of hope and the possibility of great change, even for those who would likely be written off by our own human judgment. Over and over, history has confirmed this possibility. There are no sinners anywhere in the world who are compelled to remain as they are. They may be floundering in sin, so deeply enmeshed that they are ashamed of themselves. But the very fact that they are ashamed indicates that there is a model to which they may yet attain. It is this hope of change that keeps people alive on the earth.

Change is still possible

The second ray of hope is the prospect that while there is life, no one is "finished." Whoever you are, wherever you may be, whatever your age, you are not yet a finished product. You are still in process.

I will admit that it is our human tendency to fix certain points and consider them finishes. Take human birth for instance. The obstetrician, after exclaiming "It's a boy!" and finding the baby healthy, may say, "Now, as far as I am concerned, my role in this baby's birth is finished." He establishes a terminal point there and goes about his other concerns. During all the preceding months, he was concerned—perhaps even anxious. But the terminal point has now been reached; a healthy, normal baby has been born into the world.

But the mother of that baby does not share the doctor's viewpoint. She knows she has just given birth to a tiny new life. She is aware of the long continuing process that lies ahead. She has heard about the childhood diseases, the developmental stages. She knows the educational process ahead from the time she teaches her baby to play patty-cake until he walks out of college with a degree. It is a long continuum of shaping and fashioning.

When that son of hers is awarded his college degree, probably she and her husband will breath sighs of relief and say, "Well, we have succeeded in getting our son through college!" Parents have a tendency to put a period there and to say, "Now our responsibility is over. It is finished!"

But of course we know that for the graduate himself, it is not so much a finish as a serious new beginning. There are still many changes to come; he is still being shaped and fashioned.

Many a mother breathes a sigh of relief when her son suddenly becomes serious, settles down, gets married, establishes a home. Her sigh is really her way of saying to herself, "Now my worries are over!" But not everyone who is settled down is finished.

Parents are gratified when success comes and their boy becomes vice president of his company, drawing a big check and driving an expensive car. They smile at each other and say, "Now he is fixed. He has arrived. He is a big American businessman!" It is not easy for parents to look beyond this pleasant "finish" point.

The finish is not yet

But their son is still moving along. He will come to middle age when, as the poet said, "Gray hairs are here and there upon him." The parents comment that his graying hair really gives him a distinguished look, and they cannot conceive that things will ever really change for him.

"He has arrived," is their consolation. "He is a portly, well-proportioned businessman, an executive. He plays golf. He hunts in the fall and fishes in the spring and goes to baseball games in the summer—all the things that businessmen do. Don't worry about him. He is fixed!"

But he is a human being, and he is not fixed and will not be until his soul leaves his body. Even as an old man in his dotage, he is still going to change in some ways. The rapidity and scope of change may not be as pronounced, but there is change nevertheless.

Probably someone may wish he or she could dialogue with me right here and say, "Yes, all that is true in terms of humanity—unregenerate humanity. But I do know a finish point. It is the time when a person is converted to Christ."

I will agree—partially. There is a point when we say with the song writer, "Now rest my long-divided heart, / Fixed on this blissful center, rest!" But does our conversion to Christ and our assurance of forgiveness mean that the malleability in our nature is gone and that we are finally "fixed"? The answer, I insist, is "No!" We are still malleable. We are still subject to being changed and shaped. God expects that we will grow and develop in maturity and Christlikeness. When Peter wrote, "Do not conform to the evil desires you had when you lived in ignorance," he was recognizing that Christians are still in process.

I fear there are many so-called followers of Christ who have never understood that the Christian life is a process. Perhaps Christian workers are at fault. We work so hard to get people converted that once it happens, we are inclined to put a period right there. We say to the convert, "Now rest your long-divided heart!"

Conversion is not a terminal point

There is a sense in which that old gospel song is

beautifully, brilliantly true, and I love it and sing it often. But I am sure that the writer was not intending to imply that conversion was a terminal point. He was not suggesting that the believer is no longer malleable. The fact is, he was assuring us that our being fixed in Christ is settled by an act of faith— and that is absolutely true. But when it comes to the shaping and developing, the growth and enlargement—these begin in the spiritual sense after we are converted!

I suspect someone else would like to raise an objection and insist that Christians cannot conform themselves. "God must do the conforming. He is our Heavenly Father. He must do the molding, the changing."

Let me agree this far: that is the ideal. That is the way it *should* be. If believers could be completely and wholly surrendered from the moment they are saved until the time they die, knowing nothing but the influences of God and the heavenly powers at work within them, then that would be true. But even in the kingdom of God there are other than divine powers that shape people.

Let me illustrate. Here is a young fellow interested in getting a sun tan. So he exposes himself to the sun at the beach or in his own back yard. Now, what or who is tanning his skin? Where is the tan coming from? What does the fellow himself have to do with it?

There is a sense in which the fellow himself is doing the tanning, for if he had kept his shirt on, his skin would not tan. But there is a sense in which the sun is doing the work. The sun is tanning him, but the fellow had to take the necessary steps to cooperate with the rays of the sun.

That is exactly what we mean when we say that we "conform." We conform by exposing ourselves to the divine powers that shape us. A fellow may wear his jacket and never get a tan, even though the sun is up there brightly in view. Just so, we Christians may keep ourselves wrapped in our own stubbornness and never receive the beneficial graces that filter down from God's throne where Jesus sits as Mediator.

Yes, it is possible for Christians to go through life without very much change taking place. Converted? Yes. Believers in Christ? Yes. Having the seed of God within them? Yes. But such believers are infantile. The growth and development, the beautifying and shaping have not taken place because they refuse to cooperate—to expose themselves to the divine powers designed to shape believers.

Exposure can be negative, also

The reverse side of this proposition must also be considered. It is entirely possible for Christian believers to shape themselves by exposure to the wrong kind of influences. I suspect this is happening to an extent that must indeed grieve God.

What about these powers that can shape us? We know full well what the old powers were. Those old powers were the "evil desires" we had when we lived "in ignorance." The apostle Paul soberly reminds us of those powers in his letter to the Ephesians:

You were dead in your transgressions and sins,

in which you used to live when you followed the ways of this world and of the ruler of the kingdom of the air, the spirit who is now at work in those who are disobedient. All of us also lived among them at one time, gratifying the cravings of our sinful nature and following its desires and thoughts. Like the rest, we are by nature objects of wrath. (2:1–3)

Those were the forces that had a part in shaping us in our past. But now we have come to the Savior and found in Him a resting place. Therefore, we are encouraged to put behind us those old influences. We are not to expose ourselves to them any more.

But another question comes up. "How can I hold myself from being shaped by evil influences? I am thrown daily among the people of this world. I work in a situation where my fellow workers are vulgar, obscene and wicked."

Here is my answer: If that is your situation, you must engage your own will in the direction of God's will for your life. You can keep yourself from being shaped by your situation just as a fellow in the sun can keep himself from being tanned. You can draw yourself up in faith and by an act of your will you can take a positive stand against those influences. You can say, "Stay out, you devilish influences, in the name of my Savior! Let my soul alone—it belongs to God!"

These young people have turned the tables

Young people are beset by dirty talk and irreverence and every kind of temptation in their schools. I know of Christian young people who have found a way to turn those things to personal spiritual blessing. Hearing an obscenity, they have an instant reaction and a compensation within: "Oh, God, I hate that kind of talk so much that I want You to make my own mind and speech cleaner than it ever was before!" Seeing an injurious, wicked habit in others, they breathe a silent prayer: "Oh, God, You are able to keep me and shield me from that bad habit!"

It is possible, even in this sensual world with its emphasis on violence and immorality to turn those very influences in the direction of God's promised victory. We are assured in the Word of God that we do not have to yield in weakness to the pull that would drag us down. When we see something that we know is wrong and therefore displeasing to God, we can react to it with a positive assurance as we say, "God helping me, I will be different from that!" In that sense, the very sight of evil can drive us farther into the kingdom of God.

Now, what can we put into practice from this approach? I share with you a few very simple thoughts about basic things in our own day that have powers to shape us, whether or not we are Christians. These are everyday things, and they have influence upon our lives, whether we know it or not, whether we believe it or not, whether we like it or not.

What can be said about the books and magazines you read? What you read will shape you by slowly conditioning your mind. Little by little, even though you think you are resisting, you will take on the shape of the mind of the author of that book you are reading. You will begin to put your emphasis where he puts his. You will begin to put your values where she places hers. You will find yourself liking what he likes, thinking as she thinks.

The same is certainly true of the power of modern films. If you give yourself over to their influences, they will shape your mind and your morals.

What about the music you enjoy? It seems almost too late in these times to try to warn against what many in our society seem to revel in—the vile, vicious, obscene gutter language of so much popular music. It is not overstating the case to insist that the kinds of music you enjoy will demonstrate rather accurately what you are like inside. If you give yourself to the contemporary fare of music that touches the baser emotions, it will shape your mind, your emotions, your desires, whether you admit it or not.

As a friend, I warn you

You can drink poison if you want to, but I am still friend enough to warn you that if you do, you will be carried out in a box. I cannot stop you, but I can warn you. I have not the authority to tell you what you should listen to, but I have a divine commission to tell you that if you love and listen to the wrong kinds of music, your inner life will wither and die.

What about the pleasures you indulge in. If I should start to catalog some of your pastimes, you would probably break in and ask, "What's wrong with this?" "What's wrong with that?" There probably is no answer that will completely satisfy you if you are asking the question. But this is my best answer: Give a person ten years in the wrong kind of indulgence and questionable atmosphere, and see what happens to the inward spiritual life.

The pleasures in which we indulge selfishly will shape us and fashion us over the years. Whatever gives us pleasure has the subtle power to change us and enslave us.

What are the fond ambitions you entertain for your life? The dream of whatever you would like to be will surely influence and shape you. It will also tend to determine the places where you spend your time. I realize I am not going to be very successful in advising you where you should and should not go. Just the same, if you are on your way to heaven through faith in God's Son and God's salvation plan, you should be careful about the kind of places you frequent. These will shape you and leave their imprint on your spirit and soul.

What kind of words do you speak? Of all the people in the world, I think Americans must be the most careless with language and expression. For instance, any typical American joke is an exaggeration. Mark Twain popularized exaggeration, and it has become an accepted form not only of comedy but of communication among Americans. Are you watching your own language? Are you careful of your own expressions in view of what they could mean to the effectiveness of your Christian testimony?

Who are your friends?

Who are your friends? It is important to make and cherish the right kind of friends.

I value friendship very highly. We can appreciate and honor one another in friendship, whether or

not the other person is a believer. Because it is possible that friendships can be beautiful and helpful,
I have always felt something like a churlish heel to
insist that certain friendships must be broken off if
you want to truly serve God. But our Lord Jesus
said it more bluntly than I ever could say it. He told
us that in being His disciples we must take up our
cross and follow Him. He said there would be instances when we must forsake those who would
hold us back—even if they were our own relatives
and close friends. Jesus Christ must be first in your
heart and mind. It is He who reminds you that the
salvation of your soul is of prime importance.

Better to have no friends and be an Elijah, alone,
than to be like Lot in Sodom, surrounded by
friends who all but damned him. If you give your
cherished friendship to the ungodly counsellor and
the mocker, you have given the enemy the key to
your heart. You have opened the gate, and the city
of your soul will be overwhelmed and taken!

Finally, what kind of thoughts do you spend your
time brooding over? Most murders, robberies, em-
bezzlements and other evil deeds were preceded
by long hours of brooding over the idea, making
plans, relishing the hope of revenge, savoring the
chance for gain. Whatever thoughts you brood over
in the night seasons will shape you. The thoughts
you entertain can change you from what you are
into something else. The change will not be for the
better unless your thoughts are good thoughts.

"Do not conform . . . be transformed"

In the light of all these influences, the apostle
Paul appeals to you: "Do not conform any longer to

the pattern of this world, but be transformed by the renewing of your mind. Then you will be able to test and approve what God's will is—his good, pleasing and perfect will" (Romans 12:2). You have an eternal soul. You have influences that will shape you. God gives clay to the potter and says, "Now, shape it!" God gives material to the builder and says, "Now, make a worthy temple!" Someday He will ask you what you did with and about the forces and influences that came into your daily life.

I trust that in that last great day of reckoning, you will not stand before the judgment seat of Christ and confess with shame that you allowed unworthy things to shape your life. Rather, it is time now to "be transformed by the renewing of your mind . . . to test and approve . . . God's . . . good, pleasing and perfect will."

"Just as he who called you is holy, so be holy in all you do."

The Second Coming: Our Blessed Hope

After he said this, [Jesus] was taken up before their very eyes, and a cloud hid him from their sight.

They were looking intently up into the sky as he was going, when suddenly two men dressed in white stood beside them. "Men of Galilee," they said, "why do you stand here looking into the sky? This same Jesus, who has been taken from you into heaven, will come back in the same way you have seen him go into heaven." (Acts 1:9–11)

AMID ALL THE WORLD RELIGIONS, only Christianity is able to proclaim the Bible's good news that God, the Creator and Redeemer, will bring a new order into being! Indeed, that is the only good news available to a fallen race today. God has promised a new order that will be of eternal duration and infused with eternal life.

How amazing!

It is a promise from God of a new order to be based upon the qualities the exact opposite of mankind's universal blight—temporality and mortality. God promises the qualities of perfection and eternity—qualities that cannot now be found anywhere on this earth.

What a prospect!

We are instructed that this new order, at God's bidding, will finally show itself in a new heaven and a new earth. It will show itself in a city that is to come down as a bride adorned for her husband. And it will be of eternal duration. It will not come just to go again. It is not temporal. It is a new order that will come to stay.

God in His revelation to mankind makes it very plain that the risen Christ is the Head of this new creation and that His church is the body. It is a simple picture—individual believers in the risen Christ are the body's members. This is revealed so clearly in the Bible that anyone can see and comprehend it. The whole picture is there for us to consider.

The first Adam and the old order

The first Adam—the old Adam—was the head of everything in the old order. When he fell, he pulled everything down with him. I know there are some bright people who argue against the historicity of the fall of humankind in Adam and Eve. But no person, however brilliant, wise and well-schooled, has been able to escape two brief sentences written across all of his prospects by the great God Almighty. Those two sentences are: "You cannot stay—you must go!" and "You cannot live—you must die."

No human being, regardless of talent, possessions and status, has yet won a final victory over the universal sentence of temporality and mortality. Temporality says, "You must go!" Mortality says, "You must die!"

As is man, so are his works. The same twofold blight that rests upon our sinful, fallen race—temporality and mortality—rests upon every work that mankind does.

Mankind has many areas of life and culture of which he is proud. He has long used such words as *beauty, nobility, creativity,* and *genius* to describe these efforts. But however noble these works may be, however inspired by genius, however beautiful and creative, still they have these two sentences written across them: "You cannot stay!" and "You cannot live." God reminds fallen men and women: "You came only to go, and you came surely to die!"

Everything and anything, whether a sonnet or an oratorio, a modern bridge or a great canal, a famous painting or the world's greatest novel—every one has God's twin mark of judgment upon it: temporality and mortality. Not one can remain. All are in the process of dying. All man's works share that double sentence imposed on man.

But a second Man, the new and last Adam, came into this world to bring the promise of a new and eternal order for God's creation. The Son of Man, Christ Jesus the Lord, came and died. But rising from the grave, He lives forever that He might be the Head of the new creation.

God's revelation says that Jesus Christ is the eternal Victor, triumphant over sin and death. That is why He is the Head of the new creation which has upon it the banner of eternity rather than of temporality and the mark of life forevermore rather than the mark of death.

Still, mankind resists

Throughout all the ebb and flow of world history, mankind has been totally unable to thwart the reality of death and judgment. It seems, therefore, incredible that proud men and women—both in the church and out—refuse to give heed to the victorious eternal plan and program of Jesus Christ.

Most of the reasons for the neglect of Christ's promises are all too evident among us today. For one thing, we are too impatient to wait for the promises of God. We take the short-range view of things. Our lives are surrounded by gadgets that get things done in a hurry. We have been brought up on quick oats, we like—or at least tolerate—instant coffee, we wear drip-dry shirts and blouses, we take 60-second Polaroid snapshots of our children. We buy our spring clothes before the autumn leaves fall to the ground. If we purchase a new car after July 1, it is already an old model when we drive it home. We are always in a hurry. We cannot bear to wait for anything.

This breathless way of living naturally makes for a mentality impatient of delay. And when we enter the kingdom of God through the experience of salvation, we bring this short-range psychology with us. We find prophecy too slow for our dispositions. Our first radiant expectations soon lose their luster. We are likely, then, to inquire, "Lord, are you at this time going to restore the kingdom to Israel?" And when there is no immediate response, we are inclined to conclude, "My Master is taking a long time in coming."

Actually, it has taken some people a long time to

discover that the faith of Christ offers no buttons to push for quick service. The new order must wait for the Lord's own time—and that is too much for the person in a hurry. He or she gives up and turns to other interests.

Also, there is little question but that the prevailing affluence of our society has much to do with the general disregard of Christ's promises that He will come to earth again to intervene in human history. If the rich man enters the kingdom of God with difficulty, then it is logical to conclude that a society having the highest percentage of well-to-do persons will have the lowest percentage of Christians, all other things being equal.

Fruitless preaching, unprepared saints

If the "deceitfulness of wealth" (Matthew 13:22) chokes the Word and makes it unfruitful, then this would be the day of near-fruitless preaching, at least in the opulent West. And if "dissipation, drunkenness and the anxieties of life" (Luke 21:34) tend to unfit the Christian for the coming of Christ, then this generation of Christians should be the least prepared for that event.

On the North American continent, Christianity has become the religion of the prosperous middle and upper-middle classes almost entirely; the very rich and the very poor rarely become practicing Christians. That touching picture of the shabbily dressed, hungry saint, Bible clutched under his or her arm, the light of God shining in his or her face, hobbling painfully toward the church building is largely imaginary.

Probably the most irritating problem faced by today's western Christians is where to find parking for their shiny automobiles that transported them effortlessly to the house of God, where they hope to prepare their souls for the world to come. In the United States and Canada the middle class today possesses more earthly goods and lives in greater luxury than emperors and Maharajahs did only a century ago.

Since the bulk of Christians comes from this class, it is not difficult to see why the genuine expectation of Christ's return has all but disappeared from among us. About that there can be little argument. It is hard indeed to focus attention on a better world to come when a more comfortable one than this can hardly be imagined. As long as science can make us so cozy in this present world, it is admittedly hard to work up much pleasurable anticipation of a new world order, even if it is God who has promised it.

Beyond these conditions in society, however, is the theological problem. Too many people hold an inadequate view of Jesus Christ Himself. Ours is the age in which Christ has been explained, humanized, demoted. Many professing Christians no longer expect Him to usher in a new order. They are not at all sure that He is able to do so; or if He does, it will be with the help of art, education, science and technology—that is, with the help of man. This revised expectation amounts to disillusionment for many. And, of course, no one can become too radiantly happy over a King of kings who has been stripped of His crown or a Lord of lords who has lost His sovereignty.

The teachers cannot agree

Still another facet of the problem is the continuing confusion among teachers of prophecy, some of whom seem to profess to know more than the prophets they claim to teach. This may be in the realm of history, but in the first two or three decades of the 20th century there was a feeling among evangelical Christians that the end of the age was near. There was anticipation and hope that a new world order would soon emerge. This new order was to be preceded by a silent return of Christ to earth, not to remain, but to raise the righteous dead to immortality and to glorify the living saints in the twinkling of an eye. These He would catch away to the marriage supper of the Lamb, while the earth meanwhile was plunged into its baptism of fire and blood in the Great Tribulation. This period of tribulation would be relatively brief, ending dramatically with the battle of Armageddon and the triumphant return of Christ with His bride—the church—to reign a thousand years.

Let me assure you that those expectant Christians had something very wonderful that is largely lacking today. They had a unifying hope. Their activities were concentrated. They fully expected to win. Today, our Christian hope has been subjected to so much examination, analysis and revision that we are embarrassed to admit that we believe there is genuine substance to the hope we espouse. Today, professing Christians are on the defensive, trying to prove things that a previous generation never doubted. We have allowed unbelievers to get us in a corner. We have even given them the advantage by permitting them to choose the time and place of encounter.

Today we smart under the attack of the quasi-Christian unbeliever, and the nervous, self-conscious defense we make is called "religous dialogue." Under the scornful attack of the religous critic, real Christians, who ought to know better, are now "rethinking" their faith. Worst of all, adoration has given way to celebration in the holy place—if indeed any holy place remains to this generation of confused Christians.

Doctrine versus blessed hope

In summary, I think we must note that there is a vast difference between the doctrine of Christ's coming and the hope of His coming. It surely is possible to hold the doctrine without feeling a trace of the blessed hope. Indeed, there are multitudes of Christians today who hold the doctrine. What I have tried to center on here is that overwhelming sense of anticipation that lifts the life upward to a new plane and fills the heart with rapturous optimism. This is largely lacking among us now.

Frankly, I do not know whether or not it is possible to recapture the spirit of anticipation that animated the early Christian church and cheered the hearts of gospel Christians only a few decades ago. Certainly scolding will not bring it back, nor arguing over minor points of prophecy, nor condemning those who do not agree with us. We may do any or all of these things without arousing the desired spirit of joyous expectation. That unifying, healing, purifying hope is for the childlike, the innocent-hearted, the unsophisticated.

Let me say finally that all those expectant believers in the past have not been wholly wrong. They were only wrong about the time. They saw Christ's triumph as being nearer than it was, and for that reason their timing was off. But their hope itself was valid.

Many of us have had the experience of misjudging the distance of a mountain toward which we were traveling. The huge bulk that loomed against the sky seemed very near, and it was hard to persuade ourselves that it was not receding as we approached it. So the City of God appears so large to the minds of world-weary pilgrims that they are sometimes the innocent victims of an optical illusion. They may be more than a little disappointed when the glory seems to move farther away as they approach. But the mountain is really there. They need only press on to reach it.

And the hope of these pilgrims is substance, too. Their judgment is not always too sharp, but they are not mistaken in the long view. They will see the glory in God's own time!